Criticism in America

Criticism in America
Its Function and Status

Essays by

Irving Babbitt, Van Wyck Brooks, W. C. Brownell,
Ernest Boyd, T. S. Eliot, H. L. Mencken,
Stuart P. Sherman, J. E. Spingarn,
and George E. Woodberry

New York
Harcourt, Brace and Company

PRINTED IN THE U. S. A. BY
THE QUINN & BODEN COMPANY
RAHWAY, N. J.

Prefatory Note

In the last twelve or fifteen years, side by side with the so-called "poetic Renaissance," there has developed what is probably the first fundamental discussion of the nature of criticism in American literature. The purpose of this volume is to bring together some of the more important essays representative of this discussion. The collection is not intended to be representative in any other way. The first essay dates from 1910, the last from 1923, and virtually every critical point of view is given a hearing. For permission to reprint, thanks are due to the authors of the various essays and to Messrs. Henry Holt & Co., Charles Scribner's Sons, Alfred A. Knopf, B. W. Huebsch, the Columbia University Press, and the editors of the *Nation*. The essays, several of which have been revised by their authors for this collection, are here arranged in chronological order.

25818

Contents

Criticism in America

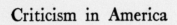

The New Criticism [1]

By J. E. SPINGARN

"What droll creatures these college professors are whenever they talk about art," wrote Flaubert in one of his letters, and voiced the world's opinion of academic criticism. For the world shares the view of the Italian poet that "monks and professors cannot write the lives of poets," and looks only to those rich in literary experience for its opinions on literature. But the poets themselves have had no special grudge against academic criticism that they have not felt equally for every other kind. For the most part, they have objected to all criticism, since what each mainly seeks in his own case is not criticism, but uncritical praise. "Kill the dog, he is a reviewer," cried the young Goethe; and in an age nearer our own William Morris expressed his contempt for

[1] A lecture delivered at Columbia University on March 9, 1910; first published by the Columbia University Press in 1911; reprinted in *Creative Criticism: Essays on the Unity of Genius and Taste* (Henry Holt & Company) in 1917.

those who earn a livelihood by writing their opinions of the works of others. Fortunately for Criticism, it does not live by the grace of poets, to whom it can be of small service at its best, but by the grace of others who have neither the poet's genius nor the critic's insight. I hope to persuade you this evening that the poets have been mistaken in their very conception of the critic's craft, which lives by a power that poets and critics share together. The secret of this power has come to men slowly, and the knowledge they have gained by it has transformed their idea of Criticism. What this secret is, and into what new paths Criticism is being led by it, is the subject of my lecture to-night.

I

At the end of the last century, France once more occupied the center of that stage whose auditors are the inheritors of European civilization. Once more all the world listened while she talked and played, and some of the most brilliant of her talk was now on the question of the authority of Criticism. It is not

The New Criticism

my purpose to tell you (what you know already) with what sober and vigorous learning the official critics of the *Revue des deux Mondes* espoused the cause of old gods with the new weapons of science, and with what charm and tact, with what grace and suppleness of thought, Jules Lemaître and Anatole France, to mention no others, defended the free play of the appreciative mind. Some of the sparks that were beaten out on the anvil of controversy have become fixed stars, the classical utterances of Criticism, as when Anatole France described the critic not as a judge imposing sentence, but as a sensitive soul detailing his "adventures among masterpieces."

To have sensations in the presence of a work of art and to express them, that is the function of Criticism for the impressionistic critic. His attitude he would express somewhat in this fashion: "Here is a beautiful poem, let us say Shelley's *Prometheus Unbound*. To read it is for me to experience a thrill of pleasure. My delight in it is itself a judgment, and what better judgment is it possible for me to give? All that I can do is to tell how it affects me, what sensations it gives me. Other men will

11

derive other sensations from it, and express them differently; they too have the same right as I. Each of us, if we are sensitive to impressions and express ourselves well, will produce a new work of art to replace the work which gave us our sensations. That is the art of Criticism, and beyond that Criticism cannot go."

We shall not begrudge this exquisite soul the pleasure of his sensations or his cult of them, nor would he be disconcerted if we were to point out that the interest has been shifted from the work of art to his own impressions. Let us suppose that you say to him: "We are not interested in you, but in *Prometheus Unbound*. To describe the state of your health is not to help us to understand or to enjoy the poem. Your criticism constantly tends to get away from the work of art, and to center attention on yourself and your feelings."

But his answer would not be difficult to find: "What you say is true enough. My criticism tends to get farther and farther from the work of art and to cast a light upon myself; but all criticism tends to get away from

the work of art and to substitute something
in its place. The impressionist substitutes
himself, but what other form of criticism gets
closer to *Prometheus Unbound?* Historical
criticism takes us away from it in a search of
the environment, the age, the race, the poetic
school of the artist; it tells us to read the history of the French Revolution, Godwin's *Political Justice*, the *Prometheus Bound* of
Æschylus, and Calderón's *Mágico Prodigioso.*
Psychological criticism takes me away from
the poem, and sets me to work on the biography of the poet; I wish to enjoy *Prometheus
Unbound*, and instead I am asked to become
acquainted with Shelley the man. Dogmatic
criticism does not get any closer to the work
of art by testing it according to rules and
standards; it sends me to the Greek dramatists,
to Shakespeare, to Aristotle's *Poetics*, possibly
to Darwin's *Origin of Species*, in order that
I may see how far Shelley has failed to give
dramatic reality to his poem, or has failed to
observe the rules of his *genre;* but that means
the study of other works, and not of *Prometheus Unbound.* Esthetics takes me still farther afield into speculations on art and beauty.

13

J. E. Spingarn

And so it is with every form of Criticism. Do not deceive yourself. All criticism tends to shift the interest from the work of art to something else. The other critics give us history, politics, biography, erudition, metaphysics. As for me, I re-dream the poet's dream, and if I seem to write lightly, it is because I have awakened, and smile to think I have mistaken a dream for reality. I at least strive to replace one work of art by another, and art can only find its *alter ego* in art."

It would be idle to detail the arguments with which the advocates of the opposing forms of Criticism answered these questionings. Literary erudition and evolutionary science were the chief weapons used to fight this modern heresy, but the one is an unwieldy and the other a useless weapon in the field of esthetic thought. On some sides, at least, the position of the impressionists was impregnable; but two points of attack were open to their opponents. They could combat the notion that taste is a substitute for learning, or learning a substitute for taste, since both are vital for Criticism; and they could maintain that the relativity of taste does not in any sense affect its authority. In this sense impressionistic Criticism erred only less grievously than the "judicial" Criticism which opposed it. Each in its own way was inadequate and incomplete.

But these arguments are not my present concern; what I wish to point out is that the objective and dogmatic forms of Criticism were fighting no new battle against impressionistic Criticism in that decade of controversy. It was a battle as old as the earliest reflection on the subject of poetry, if not as old as the sensitiveness of poets. Modern literature begins with the same doubts, with the same quarrel. In the sixteenth century the Italians were formulating that classical code which imposed itself on Europe for two centuries, and which, even in our generation, Brunetière has merely disguised under the trappings of natural science. They evolved the dramatic unities, and all those rules which the poet Pope imagined to be "Nature still but Nature methodized." But at the very moment when their spokesman Scaliger was saying that "Aristotle is our emperor, the perpetual dictator of all the fine arts," another Italian, Pietro Aretino, was in-

sisting that there is no rule except the whim
of genius and no standard of judgment beyond individual taste.

The Italians passed on the torch to the
French of the seventeenth century, and from
that day to this the struggle between the two
schools has never ceased to agitate the progress
of Criticism in France. Boileau against Saint-
Evremond, Classicists against Romanticists,
dogmatists against impressionists,—the antin-
omy is deep in the French nature, indeed in
the nature of Criticism itself. Listen to this:
"It is not for the purpose of deciding on the
merit of this noble poet [Virgil], nor of harm-
ing his reputation, that I have spoken so freely
concerning him. The world will continue to
think what it does of his beautiful verses;
and as for me, I judge nothing, I only say
what I think, and what effect each of these
things produces on my heart and mind."
Surely these words are from the lips of Lemaître himself! "I judge nothing; I only say
what I feel." But no, these are the utterances
of the Chevalier de Méré, a wit of the age of
Louis XIV, and he is writing to the secretary
of that stronghold of authority, the French

The New Criticism

Academy. For some men, even in the age of Boileau, criticism was nothing but an "adventure among masterpieces."

No, it is no new battle; it is the perpetual conflict of Criticism. In every age impressionism (or enjoyment) and dogmatism (or judgment) have grappled with one another. They are the two sexes of Criticism; and to say that they flourish in every age is to say that every age has its masculine as well as its feminine criticism,—the masculine criticism that may or may not force its own standards on literature, but that never at all events is dominated by the object of its studies; and the feminine criticism that responds to the lure of art with a kind of passive ecstasy. In the age of Boileau it was the masculine type which gave the tone to Criticism; in our own, outside of the universities, it has certainly been the feminine. But they continue to exist side by side, ever falling short of their highest powers, unless mystically mated,—judgment erecting its edicts into arbitrary standards and conventions, enjoyment lost in the mazes of its sensuous indecision.

Yet if we examine these opposing forms of

17

Criticism in our own age, we shall find, I think, that they are not wholly without a common ground to meet on; that, in fact, they are united in at least one prepossession which they do not share with the varying forms of Criticism in any of the earlier periods of its history. The Greeks conceived of literature, not as an inevitable expression of creative power, but as a reasoned "imitation" or re-shaping of the materials of life; for Aristotle, poetry is the result of man's imitative instinct, and differs from history and science in that it deals with the probable or possible rather than with the real. The Romans conceived of literature as a noble art, intended (though under the guise of pleasure) to inspire men with high ideals of life. The classicists of the sixteenth and seventeenth centuries accepted this view in the main; for them, literature was a kind of exercise,—a craft acquired by study of the classics, and guided in the interpretation of nature by the traditions of Greek and Roman art. For these men literature was as much a product of reason as science or history. The eighteenth century complicated the course of Criticism by the introduction of vague and novel criteria, such as "imagination," "sentiment," and "taste," yet it was only in part able to liberate itself from the older tradition.

But with the Romantic Movement there developed the new idea which coördinates all Criticism in the nineteenth century. Very early in the century, Mme. de Staël and others formulated the idea that literature is an "expression of society"—a phrase that is merely a half-truth if "society" is interpreted in terms of the narrow circle of the individual poet's life instead of in terms of that society which is commensurate with the spirit of man. Victor Cousin enunciated "the fundamental rule, that expression is the supreme law of art," and, as the meaning of expression was gradually misunderstood and narrowed, became the unwitting parent of the mechanical theories of the French school of "art for art's sake." Later, Sainte-Beuve developed and illustrated his theory that literature is an expression of personality—another misleading half-truth, if by personality is meant, not the artistic personality which unfolds itself in the work of art, but the complex of external traits which the artist exhibits in his practical life. Still later, under the influence of natural science, Taine took a hint from Hegel and elaborated the idea that literature is an expression of race, age, and environment. The extreme impressionists prefer to think of art as the exquisite expression of delicate and fluctuating sensations or impressions of life. But for all these critics and theorists, literature is an expression of something, of experience or emotion, of the external or internal, of the man himself or something outside the man; yet it is always conceived of as an art of expression. The objective, the dogmatic, the impressionistic critics of our day may set for themselves very different tasks, but the idea of expression is implicit in all they write.

French criticism has been leaning heavily on the idea of expression for a century or more, but no attempt has been made in France to understand its esthetic content, except for a few vague echoes of German thought. For the first to give philosophic precision to the theory of expression, and to found a method of Criticism based upon it, were the Germans of the age that stretches from Herder to Hegel. All the forces of philosophical thought were focused on this central concept, while the critics enriched themselves from out this golden store. I suppose you all remember the famous passage in which Carlyle describes the achievement of German criticism in that age. "Criticism," says Carlyle, "has assumed a new form in Germany. It proceeds on other principles and proposes to itself a higher aim. The main question is not now a question concerning the qualities of diction, the coherence of metaphors, the fitness of sentiments, the general logical truth in a work of art, as it was some half century ago among most critics, neither is it a question mainly of a psychological sort to be answered by discovering and delineating the peculiar nature of the poet from his poetry, as is usual with the best of our own critics at present; but it is, not indeed exclusively, but inclusively, of its two other questions, properly and ultimately a question of the essence and peculiar life of the poetry itself. . . . The problem is not now to determine by what mechanism Addison composed sentences and struck out similitudes, but by what far finer and more mysterious mechanism Shakespeare organized his dramas and

21

gave life and individuality to his Ariel and
his Hamlet. Wherein lies that life; how have
they attained that shape and individuality?
Whence comes that empyrean fire which ir-
radiates their whole being, and pierces, at least
in starry gleams, like a diviner thing, into all
hearts? Are these dramas of his not veri-
similar only, but true; nay, truer than reality
itself, since the essence of unmixed reality is
bodied forth in them under more expressive
similes? What is this unity of pleasures; and
can our deeper inspection discern it to be in-
divisible and existing by necessity because each
work springs as it were from the general elements of thought and grows up therefrom into
form and expansion by its own growth? Not
only who was the poet and how did he compose, but what and how was the poem, and
why was it a poem and not rhymed eloquence,
creation and not figured passion? These are
the questions for the critic. Criticism stands
like an interpreter between the inspired and
the uninspired; between the prophet and those
who hear the melody of his words, and catch
some glimpse of their material meaning, but
understand not their deeper import."

The New Criticism

I am afraid that no German critic wholly
realized this ideal; but it was at least the
achievement of the Germans that they enunciated the doctrine, even if they did not always
adequately illustrate it in practice. It was
they who first realized that art has performed
its function when it has expressed itself; it
was they who first conceived of Criticism as
the study of expression. "There is a destructive and a creative or constructive criticism,"
said Goethe; the first measures and tests literature according to mechanical standards, the
second answers the fundamental questions:
"What has the writer proposed to himself to
do? and how far has he succeeded in carrying
out his own plan?" Carlyle, in his essay on
Goethe, almost uses Goethe's own words, when
he says that the critic's first and foremost duty
is to make plain to himself "what the poet's
aim really and truly was, how the task he had
to do stood before his eye, and how far, with
such materials as were afforded him, he has
fulfilled it."

This has been the central problem, the guiding star, of all modern criticism. From Coleridge to Pater, from Sainte-Beuve to Lemaître,

23

this is what critics have been striving for, even when they have not succeeded; yes, even when they have been deceiving themselves into thinking that they were striving for something else. This was not the ideal of the critics of Aristotle's day, who, like so many of their successors, censured a work of art as "irrational, impossible, morally hurtful, self-contradictory, or contrary to technical correctness." This was not Boileau's standard when he blamed Tasso for the introduction of Christian rather than pagan mythology into epic poetry; nor Addison's, when he tested *Paradise Lost* according to the rules of Le Bossu; nor Dr. Johnson's, when he lamented the absence of poetic justice in *King Lear*, or pronounced dogmatically that the poet should not "number the streaks of the tulip." What has the poet tried to do, and how has he fulfilled his intention? What is he striving to express and how has he expressed it? What vital and essential spirit animates his work, what central impression does it leave on the receptive mind, and how can I best express this impression? Is his work true to the laws of its own being rather than to laws formulated by

24

others? These are the questions that modern critics have been taught to ask when face to face with the work of a poet. Only one *caveat* must be borne in mind when attempting to answer them; the poet's aim must be judged at the moment of the creative act, that is to say, by the art of the poem itself, and not by the vague ambitions which he imagines to be his real intentions before or after the creative act is achieved. For to create a work of art is the goal of every artist; and all questions in regard to his achievement resolve themselves into this: Has he or has he not created a work of art?

II

The theory of expression, the concept of literature as an art of expression, is the common ground on which critics have met for a century or more. Yet how many absurdities, how many complicated systems, how many confusions have been superimposed on this fundamental idea; and how slowly has its full significance become the possession of critics! To accept the naked principle is to play havoc with these confusions and complications; and no one has seen this more clearly, or driven home its inevitable consequences with more intelligence and vigor, than an Italian thinker and critic of our own day, Benedetto Croce, who has been gaining ground in the English-speaking world from the day when Mr. Balfour several years ago gave him a kind of official introduction in his Romanes Lecture. But I for one needed no introduction to his work; under his banner I enrolled myself long ago, and here re-enroll myself in what I now say. He has led esthetic thought inevitably from the concept that art is expression to the conclusion that all expression is art. Time does not permit, nor reason ask, that we should follow this argument through all its *pros* and *cons*. If this theory of expression be once and for all accepted, as indeed it has been partly though confusedly accepted by all modern critics, the ground of Criticism is cleared of its dead lumber and its weeds. I propose now merely to point out this dead lumber and these weeds. In other words, we shall see to what conclusions the critical thought and practice of a century have been inevitably converging,

and what elements of the old Criticism and
the old literary history are disappearing from
the new.

In the first place, we have done with all
the old Rules. The very conception of "rules"
harks back to an age of magic, and reminds
the modern of those mysterious words which
the heroes of the fairy-tales are without reason
forbidden to utter; the rules are a survival of
the savage *taboo*. We find few arbitrary rules
in Aristotle, who limited himself to empirical
inductions from the experience of literature;
but they appear in the later Greek rhetoricians;
and in the Romans, empirical induction has
been hardened into dogma. Horace lays down
the law to the prospective playwright in this
manner: "You must never have more than
three actors on the stage at any one time;
you must never let your drama have more or
less than five acts." It is unnecessary to trace
the history of these rules, or to indicate how
they increased in number, how they were
arranged into a system by the classicists of
the sixteenth and seventeenth centuries, and
how they burdened the creative art of that
period. They were never without thir ene-

mies. We have seen how Aretino was pitted against Scaliger, Saint-Evremond against Boileau; and in every age the poets have astounded the critics by transgressing rules without the sacrifice of beauty; but it was not until the end of the eighteenth century that the Romanticists banished them from the province of Criticism. The pedantry of our own day has borrowed "conventions" from history and "technique" from science as substitutes for the outworn formulæ of the past; but these are merely new names for the old mechanical rules; and they too will go, when Criticism clearly recognizes in every work of art a spiritual creation governed by its own law.

We have done with the *genres*, or literary kinds. Their history is inseparably bound up with that of the classical rules. Certain works of literature have a general resemblance and are loosely classed together (for the sake of convenience) as lyric, comedy, tragedy, epic, pastoral, and the like; the classicists made of each of these divisions a fixed norm governed by inviolable laws. The separation of the *genres* was a consequence of this law of clas-

The New Criticism

sicism: comedy should not be mingled with
tragedy, nor epic with lyric. But no sooner
was the law enunciated than it was broken
by an artist impatient or ignorant of its re-
straints, and the critics have been obliged to
explain away these violations of their laws,
or gradually to change the laws themselves.
But if art is organic expression, and every work
of art is to be interrogated with the question,
"What has it expressed, and how completely?"
there is no place for the question whether it
has conformed to some convenient classification of critics or to some law derived from
this classification. The lyric, the pastoral, the
epic, are abstractions without concrete reality
in the world of art. Poets do not really write
epics, pastorals, lyrics, however much they may
be deceived by these false abstractions; they
express themselves, and this expression is their
only form. There are not, therefore, only
three, or ten, or a hundred literary kinds; there
are as many kinds as there are individual poets.
But it is in the field of literary history that
this error is most obvious. Shakespeare wrote
King Lear, *Venus and Adonis*, and a sequence
of sonnets. What becomes of Shakespeare, the

29

creative artist, when these three works are
separated from one another by the historian
of poetry; when they lose their connection with
his single creative soul, and are classified with
other works with which they have only a loose
and vague relation? To slice up the history of English literature into compartments
marked comedy, tragedy, lyric, and the like,
is to be guilty of a complete misunderstanding of the meaning of Criticism; and literary
history becomes a logical absurdity when its
data are not organically related but cut up
into sections, and placed in such compartments
as these. Only in one sense has any of these
terms any profound significance, and that is
the use of the word "lyric" to represent the
free expressiveness of art. All art is lyrical,
—the *Divine Comedy*, *King Lear*, Rodin's
"Thinker," the Parthenon, a Corot landscape,
a Bach fugue, or Isadora Duncan's dancing, as
much as the songs of Heine or Shelley.

We have done with the comic, the tragic,
the sublime, and an army of vague abstractions of their kind. These have grown out of
the generalizations of the Alexandrian critics,
acquiring a new lease of life in the eighteenth

century. Gray and his friend West corresponded with each other on the subject of the sublime; later, Schiller distinguished between the naïve and the sentimental; Jean Paul defined humor, and Hegel defined the tragic. If these terms represent the content of art, they may be relegated to the same category as joy, hate, sorrow, enthusiasm; and we should speak of the comic in the same general way in which we might speak of the expression of joy in a poem. If, on the other hand, these terms represent abstract classifications of poetry, their use in criticism sins against the very nature of art. Every poet reexpresses the universe in his own way, and every poem is a new and independent expression. The tragic does not exist for Criticism, but only Æschylus and Calderón, Shakespeare and Racine. There is no objection to the use of the word tragic as a convenient label for somewhat similar poems, but to find laws for the tragic and to test creative artists by such laws as these is simply to give a more abstract form to the outworn classical conception of dramatic rules.

We have done with the theory of style, with

metaphor, simile, and all the paraphernalia of
Græco-Roman rhetoric. These owe their existence to the assumption that style is separate
from expression, that it is something which
may be added or subtracted at will from the
work of art, a flourish of the pen, an external
embellishment, instead of the poet's individual
vision of reality, the music of his whole
manner of being. But we know that art *is*
expression, that it is complete in itself, that
to alter it is to create another expression and
therefore to create another work of art. If
the poet, for example, says of springtime that
" 'Tis now the blood runs gold," he has not
employed a substitute for something else, such
as "the blood tingles in our veins"; he has
expressed his thought in its completeness, and
there is no equivalent for his expression except
itself.

> "Each perfect in its place; and each content   2
> With that perfection which its being meant."

Such expressions are still called metaphors in
the text-books; but metaphor, simile, and all
the old terms of classical rhetoric are signs of
the zodiac, magical incantations, astrological

formulæ, interesting only to antiquarian curiosity. To Montaigne they suggested "the
prattle of chambermaids"; to me they suggest
rather the drone and singsong of many school-
mistresses. We still hear talk of the "grand
style," and essays on style continue to be written, like the old "arts of poetry" of two centuries ago. But the theory of styles has no
longer a real place in modern thought; we have
learned that it is no less impossible to study
style as separate from the work of art than
to study the comic as separate from the work
of the comic artist.

We have done with all moral judgment of
art as art. Horace said that pleasure and
profit are the function or end of poetry, and
for many centuries the critics quarreled over
the terms "pleasure" and "profit." Some said
that poetry was meant to instruct; some,
merely to please; some, to do both. Romantic
criticism first enunciated the principle that art
has no aim except expression; that its aim is
complete when expression is complete; that
"beauty is its own excuse for being." It is
not the inherent function of poetry to further
any moral or social cause, any more than it is

the function of bridge-building to further the cause of Esperanto. The historian, the philosopher, the legislator, may consider a work of art, not as a work of art, but as a social document, just as the quarryman may consider a statue merely as so many pounds of marble, but in so doing they ignore its essential purpose and the fundamental source of its power. For if the achievement of the poet be to express any material he may select, and to express it with a completeness that we recognize as perfection, obviously morals can play no part in the judgment which Criticism may form of this artistic achievement. To say that poetry, as poetry, is moral or immoral is as meaningless as to say that an equilateral triangle is moral and an isosceles triangle immoral, or to speak of the immorality of a musical chord or a Gothic arch. It is only conceivable in a world in which dinner-table conversation runs after this fashion: "This cauliflower would be good if it had only been prepared in accordance with international law." "Do you know why my cook's pastry is so good? Because he has never told a lie or seduced a woman." We do not concern ourselves with morals when we test

The New Criticism

the engineer's bridge or the scientist's researches; indeed we go farther, and say that
it is the moral duty of the scientist to disregard
any theory of morals in his search for truth.
Beauty's world is remote from both these
standards; she aims neither at morals nor at
truth. Her imaginary creations, by definition,
make no pretense to reality, and cannot be
judged by reality's tests. The poet's only
moral duty, as a poet, is to be true to his art,
and to express his vision of reality as well as
he can. If the ideals enunciated by poets are
not those which we admire most, we must
blame not the poets but ourselves: in the world
where morals count we have failed to give
them the proper material out of which to rear
a nobler edifice. In so far as this is inherent in
the nature of our humanity, it is not affected
by the special conditions of any single society
in space and time: though art is a symbol
of the eternal conflict between aspiration and
reality, it must at the same time remain forever a symbol of mortal imperfection. Critics
everywhere except in America have ceased to
test literature by the standards of ethics, and
recognize in art an inevitable expression of a

J. E. Spingarn

side of man's nature that can find no other realization except in it.

We have done with the confusion between the drama and the theater which has permeated dramatic criticism for over half a century. The theory that the drama is not a creative art, but a mere product of the physical exigencies of the theater, is as old as the sixteenth century. An Italian scholar of that age was the first to maintain that plays are intended to be acted on a stage, under certain restricted physical conditions, and before a large and heterogeneous crowd; dramatic performance has developed out of these conditions, and the test of its excellence is therefore the pleasure it gives to the mixed audience that supports it. This idea was taken hold of by some of the German romanticists, for the purpose of justifying the Shakespearean drama in its apparent divergence from the classical "rules." Shakespeare cannot be judged by the rules of the Greek theater (so ran their argument), for the drama is an inevitable product of theatrical conditions; these conditions in Elizabethan England were not the same as those of Periclean Athens; and it is therefore absurd to

36

judge Shakespeare's practice by that of Sophocles. Here at least the idea helped to bring Shakespeare home to many new hearts by ridding the age of mistaken prejudices, and served a useful purpose, as a specious argument may persuade men to contribute to a noble work, or a mad fanatic may rid the world of a tyrant. But with this achievement its usefulness but not its life was ended. It has been developed into a system, and become a dogma of dramatic critics; it is our contemporary equivalent for the "rules" of seventeenth-century pedantry. As a matter of fact, the dramatic artist is to be judged by no other standard than that applied to any other creative artist: what has he tried to express, and how has he expressed it? It is true that the theater is not only an art but a business, and the so-called "success" of a play is of vital interest to the theater in so far as it is a commercial undertaking. "The success may justify the playwright," said an old French critic, "but it may not be so easy to justify the success." The test of "success" is an economic test, and concerns not art or the criticism of art, but political economy. Valuable contributions to economic and social

history have been made by students who have
investigated the changing conditions of the
theater and the vicissitudes of taste on the part
of theatrical audiences; but these have the
same relation to Criticism, and to the drama
as an art, that a history of the publisher's
trade and its influence on the personal fortunes of poets would bear to the history of
poetry.

We have done with technique as separate
from art. It has been pointed out that style
cannot be disassociated from art; and the false
air of science which the term "technique"
seems to possess should not blind us to the
fact that it too involves the same error.
"Technique is really personality; that is the
reason why the artist cannot teach it, why the
pupil cannot learn it, and why the esthetic
critic can understand it," says Oscar Wilde, in
a dialogue on "The Critic as Artist," which,
amid much perversity and paradox, is il-
lumined by many flashes of strange insight.
The technique of poetry cannot be separated
from its inner nature. Versification cannot
be studied by itself, except loosely and for
convenience; it remains always an inherent

quality of the single poem.   No two poets
ever write in the same metre.   Milton's line:—

"These my sky-robes spun out of Iris' woof"

is called an iambic pentameter; but it is not
true that artistically it has something in common with every other line possessing the same
succession of syllables and accents; in this sense
it is not an iambic pentameter; it is only one
thing; it is the line:—

"These my sky-robes spun out of Iris' woof."

We have done with the history and criticism
of poetic themes.   It is possible to speak
loosely of the handling of such a theme as
Prometheus by Æschylus and by Shelley, of
the story of Francesca da Rimini by Dante,
Stephen Phillips, and D'Annunzio, or the story
of King Arthur by Malory and Tennyson; but
strictly speaking, they are not employing the
same theme at all.   Each artist is expressing
a certain material and labeling it with an historic name.   For Shelley Prometheus is only a
label; he is expressing his artistic conception
of life, not the history of a Greek Titan.   It

39

J. E. Spingarn

is the vital flame he has breathed into his work that makes it what it is, and with this vital flame (and not with labels) the critic should concern himself in the works of poets. The same answer must be given to those critics who insist on the use of contemporary material in poetry, and praise the poets whose subjects are drawn from the life of our own time. But even if it were possible for critics to determine in advance the subject-matter of poetry or to impose subjects on poets, how can a poet deal with anything but contemporary material? How can a twentieth-century poet, even when he imagines that he is concerned with Greek or Egyptian life, deal with any subject but the life of his own time, except in the most external and superficial detail? Cynics have said since the first outpourings of men's hearts, "There is nothing new in art; there are no new subjects." But the very reverse is true. There are no old subjects; every subject is new as soon as it has been transformed by the imagination of the poet.

We have done with the race, the time, the environment of a poet's work as an element in Criticism. To study these phases of a work

40

The New Criticism

of art is to treat it as an historic or social document, and the result is a contribution to the history of culture or civilization, with only a subsidiary interest for the history of art. We are not here concerned with the value of such studies as empirical preparations or concomitants, but only in their relation to the essential and inherent nature of the critical act. "Granted the times, the environment, the race, the passions of the poet, what has he done with his materials, how has he converted poetry out of reality?" To answer this question of the Italian De Sanctis as it refers to each single work of art is to perform what is truly the critic's vital function; this is to interpret "expression" in its rightful sense, and to liberate esthetic Criticism from the vassalage to *Kulturgeschichte* imposed on it by the school of Taine.

We have done with the "evolution" of literature. The concept of progress was first applied to literature in the seventeenth century, but at the very outset Pascal pointed out that a distinction must here be made between science and art; that science advances by accumulation of knowledge, while the

41

changes of art cannot be reduced to any theory of progress. As a matter of fact, the theory involves the ranking of poets according to some arbitrary conception of their value; and the ranking of writers in order of merit has become obsolete, except in the "hundred best books" of the last decade and the "five-foot shelves" of yesterday. The later nineteenth century gave a new air of verisimilitude to this old theory by borrowing the term "evolution" from science; but this too involves a fundamental misconception of the free and original movement of art. A similar misconception is involved in the study of the "origins" of art; for art has no origin separate from man's life.

"In climes beyond the solar road,
  Where shaggy forms o'er ice-built mountains roam,
  The Muse has broke the twilight-gloom";

but though she wore savage raiment, she was no less the Muse. Art is simple at times, complex at others, but it is always art. The simple art of early times may be studied with profit; but the researches of anthropology have no vital significance for Criticism, unless the anthropologist studies the simplest forms of art

in the same spirit as its highest; that is, unless
the anthropologist is an esthetic critic.

Finally, we have done with the old rupture
between genius and taste. When Criticism
first propounded as its real concern the oft-
repeated question: "What has the poet tried
to express and how has he expressed it?" Criticism prescribed for itself the only possible
method. How can the critic answer this question without becoming (if only for a moment
of supreme power) at one with the creator?
That is to say, taste must reproduce the work
of art within itself in order to understand and
judge it; and at that moment esthetic judgment becomes nothing more nor less than creative art itself. The identity of genius and
taste is the final achievement of modern
thought on the subject of art, and it means
that fundamentally, in their most significant
moments, the creative and the critical instincts
are one and the same. From Goethe to Carlyle, from Carlyle to Arnold, from Arnold to
Symons, there has been much talk of the "creative function" of Criticism. For each of these
men the phrase held a different content; for
Arnold it meant merely that Criticism creates

the intellectual atmosphere of the age,—a
social function of high importance, perhaps,
yet wholly independent of esthetic significance.
But the ultimate truth toward which these men
were tending was more radical than that, and
plays havoc with all the old platitudes about
the sterility of taste. Criticism at last can
free itself of its age-long self-contempt, now
that it may realize that esthetic judgment and
artistic creation are instinct with the same vital
life. This identity does not sum up the whole
life of the complex and difficult art of Criticism; but it is this identity which has been
lost sight of and needs most emphasis now,
for without it Criticism would really be impossible. "Genius is to esthetics what the ego
is to philosophy, the only supreme and absolute
reality," said Schelling; and without subduing
the mind to this transcendental system, it remains true that what must always be inex-
plicable to mere reflection is just what gives
power to poetry; that intellectual curiosity
may amuse itself by asking its little questions
of the silent sons of light, but they vouchsafe
no answer to art's pale shadow, thought; the
gods are kind if they give up their secret in

The New Criticism

another work of art, the art of Criticism, that
serves as some sort of mirror to the art of
literature, only because in their flashes of insight taste and genius are one.

Two Phases of Criticism: *Historical and Esthetic* [1]

By GEORGE EDWARD WOODBERRY

I. *Historical Criticism*

WHAT is the act of criticism? It has lately
been succinctly described as a repetition of the
creative act of genius originating a work of
art; to criticize is to re-create. The critic is
genius at one remove; he is not unlike an actor
on the stage, and incarnates in his mind, as
the actor embodies in his person, another's
work; only thus does he understand art, realize
it, know it; and having arrived at this, his task
is done. This is the last word of modern theory. It is obvious that it simplifies the function of criticism, and relieves it apparently of
much of its old service. It relieves it, for example, of judgment; the critic understands, he

[1] Lectures delivered at Kenyon College in May, 1913;
printed by the Woodberry Society in 1914; reprinted in
The Heart of Man and Other Papers (Harcourt, Brace and
Company) in 1920. The omissions indicated by asterisks
have been made by the author for this collection.

46

does not judge. It relieves it of interpretation; the critic presents, he does not interpret. Strictly speaking, it seems a private affair that he is engaged in, an appreciation within his own consciousness; for the public to benefit by this method, every one must become his own critic, since to create or re-create is a deeply personal act. I pass no judgment on this theory now, but I shall return to it and shall endeavor to draw out its fruitful side. I desire, however, to state it at the outset, in order to throw into relief against it the matter of the present discourse, which deals with an older conception of the critic's service.

The theory whose main position I have outlined limits art narrowly to its own world, the esthetic sphere of the soul in which genius works and from which its creations proceed, a world transcending that in which human life habitually goes on, and existing by virtue of its ideality on a higher plane of being. The world of art has an absolute and eternal quality which it imparts to its creations; and one feels this the more in proportion as he has intimacy with them, enters into and lives in their world, and achieves its reality by virtue

47

George Edward Woodberry

of that union with the creative mind which
the new theory sets forth as the end of criticism.

But works of art have also a purely phenomenal side; once created, they belong to the
world of phenomena, and having come into
existence there, they are subject to the order
of time, to current human conditions, to changing judgments intellectual and moral, to varieties of fortune; in short, they are no longer
isolated and in a place of their own, the artist's
mind, but are part of a larger world. They
put on many relations, and thereby enlarge
their being; they generate new interests, and
thereby vary their significance; and the older
criticism took note of these things. In brief,
works of art take their place in time, and give
rise to a history of art. They are terms of a
temporal series; they "look before and after";
and however isolate and absolute may be their
esthetic value, they offer, to say the least, other
pertinent phases of interest, when taken as a
development in time.

The older criticism concerned itself much
with germinal origins and shaping influences,
questions of race, climate, geographical posi-

48

tion, social environment, political fortune. I
need only recall to you the brilliant mono-
graphs in which Taine made the art of the
North emanate from fog, shadow and damp,
and the art of the South weave its being of
sun, color and broad prospects, till it almost
seemed that poetry was a branch of clima-
tology, that temperature was race-tempera-
ment, war and commerce other names for epic
and comedy, and genius rather a social phenomenon than a personal power. This resolution of facts into general causes, of partic-
ularity into law, of the individual into the
mass, belonged to the bent of his mind, the
mind of a philosopher; it is naturally irritat-
ing to those who find personality to be the
fiery core of life; but his method brings out
the distinguishing features, as wholes, of the
artistic periods to which it is applied, maps
as it were their local and temporal emergence
as units of history, and displays on the background of the common *milieu* the group-traits
of each country and age. Work of all kinds
is the fruit of a partnership between man and
the world. Taine's method brings into full
view the world-factor, and by its emphasis and

preoccupation with this puts the objective element to the fore in the genesis of art.

The balance is redressed by the psychologists, who, in turn putting the subjective element in the fore, show as ardent a will to be absorbed in personality as Taine to escape from it. To them the individual is all; and not only that, but what is most peculiar and *sui generis* in him, his idiosyncrasy, is idealized as the fount and substance of his genius. Often it would seem that his title to be reckoned among the sons of light is not clear till some abnormality is discovered in him. Criticism loses itself in biography and medicine, gossip, chatter and pathology; and of late that defective, delinquent degenerate, genius, seems hunted to his lair in the subconscious self. In recent years, too, there has sprung up a third group, a hybrid of the sociologists and the psychologists, which in the name of comparative literature has constituted of the republic of letters an international state in lieu of ordinary society, and has found its controlling factors in great personalities such as Petrarch, Rousseau, Goethe, and, secondary to them, a vast network of influences working between nations and epochs; and in the hands of these scholars criticism has become an anatomy of texts.

In these various modern diversions and divagations, determined by the scientific spirit of the last century, criticism shows a temper analogous to that which at an earlier time in the scholastic world committed it to logic in the classification of the kinds of literature, epic, drama, lyric and the like and to rhetoric in the formulation of the rules. It is plain that in all such labors, ancient or modern, criticism gets ever further away from the work of art itself; it leaves the matter of life, which art is, for the matter of knowledge; and when we consider the extraordinary variety of the tasks which criticism latterly has set for itself, whatever their value and interest as matter of knowledge may be, it certainly seems time to ask whether there be not a more defined sphere, less confounded with all knowledge, for criticism to move in, and a peculiar function for that art to fulfill which in the hands of its great masters, the poets, has been an art of interpreting and manifesting life at its height of power in genius.

51

George Edward Woodberry

Shall we, then, return to the new definition? To criticize is to re-create the work of art as it was in the mind of the original artist. But how to do this? It is a simple matter to re-create from what is before us, from the image or the text, "a vision of our own"; but to require that the vision be the same that was in the mind of the artist places it at once in the field of history; it is the state of mind of a man in the past, a particular man in his own time and place, that is to be recovered. What if the work of art be that of a race different in temperament, a Persian poem, for example? or one of an unfamiliar technique, like a Japanese print? or one of an antiquated dramatic habit and a primitive morality, such as an Æschylean trilogy?

It is true that in art there is a universal element that, broadly speaking, appeals to all minds that are capable of receiving it; but in successive times it is dressed in the trappings of its own age, and attended by local and temporal associations, and though it may be interpreted in diverse tongues, it has a different tone and accent and offers a different signification in each. Just as it is necessary

to read the language before one can understand
the text, it is needful to endue the mind with
various knowledge before it can take in foreign
ideas and emotions in their original sense;
and, indeed, if one would appropriate the past,
as it was, he must put on the whole garment
of time. The end given being to realize the
state of mind of a man at a past moment—it
may be in China or Peru—the office of historical criticism seems an indispensable prelimi-
nary; and by historical criticism I mean all
those studies, sociological, psychological or
comparative, which assist in the representation
of the past, and amplify and clarify historical
knowledge. They are essential preliminaries
to that task of re-creating the work of art as
it was in the mind of the original artist. The
extent of this preparatory study, in each instance, depends upon the case in hand; but
in any case the critic must know the artist and
the world he lived in, to reproduce his mental
states with precision, or even approximately,
and this necessity bears the more heavily upon
him in proportion to the presence in the work
of art of what is alien in time, race and method.

The injunction to re-create what was in the

mind of the artist, when put forth with the
implication that historical criticism can be dispensed with, derives its plausibility from the
inveterate habit of the intellect of regarding
life not as a perpetual flux, but as fixed. This
is the mother of many practical fallacies. If
there were only the European world and our
own century, the maxim might work with sufficient success; but no sooner do we go about
the world than we find other races and civili-
zations with an art of their own which at first
view is inscrutable to us; and no sooner do
we, in our own studies, go out of our own time
and retrace the course of our own civilization
than we discover art which is equally unfamiliar and enigmatic to us, such as Byzan-
tine mosaic, for example, and primitive art
generally; and even in the literature of the
past there is much which has little or no meaning to us. History, indeed, shows us our ancestors encountering successively alien literatures and appropriating them as they became
gradually intelligible, and in each case a
Renaissance attended the appropriation—a
Celtic, Greek, Italian, Gothic Renaissance.
History unfolds such a flux, not merely of

Two Phases of Criticism

events and things in general, but of art in all its forms. But the intellect, in connection with its other systems of abstract thought conceived as fixed, has elaborated a logical scheme of art, in which all art is contained and is equally accessible to the mind. Art, however, is not thus known in the abstract like science, but only in the flux, in the concrete; that is its nature. . . .

I am not disposed to relinquish historical criticism; nay, rather I must cling to it as my only hope of qualifying myself to undertake that purely esthetic criticism by which I may at last become one with the soul of the artist and see his vision with the meaning and atmosphere it had to himself. So much of art is antique and foreign, so much of what is racially our own has become alien to my feelings and ideas by the gradual detachment of time, that I need an interpreter between me and this dead and dying world of the past—I need precisely the interpretation of knowledge that historical criticism gives. True, it is not esthetic criticism; but esthetic criticism, in the sense of a re-creation of art as it was in the past, for me is impossible without it.

George Edward Woodberry

In the same way that I cannot spare interpretation, I am reluctant also to excuse criticism from the function of judgment. It is said that the critic is concerned with two questions—"What was in the mind of the artist? Has he expressed it?" To reply to these is the whole of the critic's business. Here, again, the new theory narrowly limits the critic to the esthetic field. The intention is to debar the critic from any inquiry into the nature of what was in the artist's mind, or any examination of the means of expression employed, or any judgment upon the value of the complete work. Whether the artist's intention was one proper to his art, whether his method was well or ill adapted to its material and processes, whether the result was worth the pains, are questions that can find no place. Granted the artist's aim, has he won success? and there an end. It is assumed, you observe, that there are no rules that are binding in the art, and that the artist himself is a man utterly free, without fealty or responsibility of any sort, of whom nothing is to be required except success in working his own will. Such freedom may belong to the esthetic world, and

Two Phases of Criticism

constitute, indeed, the normal condition of life there—the artist's life; but I find these assumptions too sweeping when they are introduced into the world of criticism. I say nothing of works of art in the process of their creation, at present; but I repeat that, once created, they enter into the ordinary world of men and there they are subject to intellectual and moral values, being variously useful or harmful, as well as to analysis of their technique in the light of tradition. They have passed out of the artist's creative mind, and are part of the larger human world—a lower and different world, it may be, but one in which communal interests and values have justly a great place, often to the detriment of the sporadic individual, though an artist. In the social world, if innovation has its privileges, tradition has its rights. The rules of any craft grow out of experience; if an original and inventive artist finds novel ways, he does not, generally, altogether invalidate the old rules; most often he merely amends and improves them. The rules assume no finality; they embody past tradition, and incorporate new experience as soon as it has been warranted by success. It is true that genius is always breaking rules and with the happiest fortune; it is the critic's delight to be acknowledging instances of this constantly, for it means vitality and discovery; but breaking rules is not genius, and criticism does a very useful service generally, in such art as engraving, for example, in keeping under close observation the methods used or attempted, in the light of the tradition of the various crafts where hand and eye work together. Neither is success genius. It is still pertinent for criticism to inquire into the quality of the success, its value; and I am conservative enough to add that the critic may even ask whether it was right. Esthetic freedom is like free speech; it is, indeed, a form of free speech. We can never have too much of it. But the wisdom of what is said, the value of what is created—that is another matter; and we who find in the merely human world no guide so safe as reason, look to criticism to declare the judgment of reason on the intellectual and moral values of art.

But has art any intellectual and moral values? . . . I do not see that art, in being phenomenal, escapes from the reason any more than life does, which is also phenomenal in the same sense. The faculties of the mind work on the material of art precisely as they work on the material of life. There is this difference, however, between the two worlds of life and art, that the former is a chance medley, an arrangement that happens, while the latter is an arrangement in which the higher faculties have intervened; it is an intended arrangement. In the casual happenings of life we find tragedy and comedy, but in the art of the drama they have been freed from incongruous and confusing admixtures, and are seen in a purer form. Among the living we find beauty, but in the sculptures of the Parthenon it is unveiled to our eyes in a more apparent form. The intervention of genius has charged phenomena with something new, vital and transforming, namely, with its own personality. It is conceded, in the new theory, that the contents of the work of art, its meaning, is constituted of the artist's personality expressed therein. What a lean and diminished personality that would be from which intellectual and moral elements were excluded! . . .

George Edward Woodberry

The revolt against historical and judicial criticism, the attempt to confine the critic to an act of contemplation or simple intuition and whatever may result from that in his mind, in the belief that he will thus repeat what was in the mind of the artist, springs, I think, from a discontent with that immersion in the dead past of knowledge which is often the scholar's lot, and from a desire to confine our interest in art within those limits where art is alive. I sympathize with this discontent and this desire. It is true that in historical criticism the mind travels far from the work of art itself, and makes a long detour through biography and social and political history; and often it arrives at its true task only through linguistics and archeology. This is wearisome, especially if one is really interested in art and letters. It is true also that in analyzing the contents of epic and drama, tales of chivalry, Eastern fables and Northern sagas, the mind is dealing often with dead intellect and dead morals, with antiquated methods, with what was inchoate in the primitive and decaying in the overripe; in a word, with what belongs in the tomb, from which as a matter of fact much of it comes. But that is the lot of the scholar. "My days among the dead are passed," is the inscription over his Inferno. But if one insists on re-creating in his own mind precisely what was in the mind of the original artist—or, since that is confessedly hopeless, on approximating that ideal as closely as possible—then, I see no help for it. History is a thing of the dead past. It is an embalmment, wearing a mummified resemblance to life. Many are the voices in our time, beginning with Emerson, that have cried, "Away with it!" "Let us sweep our houses clean of death," they say, "and have only life for a housemate." There is a group of young men in Italy who advocate the destruction of the art of the past there; they say that it is in the way. If anything in the past is worth preserving, surely it is the history of the soul, and if any history is worth knowing, it is that history. Any pains that any scholar may be put to, in acquiring that knowledge, is worth while; but, after all, death enters also into the history of the soul, and much that is recorded there is no longer vital, no longer of this world. Yet it is true in realizing the dead selves of mankind, the soul accumulates power, breadth of outlook, tolerance and especially, I think, faith and hope. The scholar who accumulates in himself the human past has something of that wisdom which goes, in individual life, with a long memory. This is the service of historical criticism, that it stores and vivifies memory: it is a great service, and I would not dispense with it; but, especially in the world of art, which is the most intense realm of life, one is often fain to ask—"Is there no rescue from this reign of death, which is history, and how shall it be accomplished?"

II. *Esthetic Criticism*

Is it an error to relegate art to the dead past and translate it into history? Works of art are not like political events and persons; they do not pass at once away. The Hermes of Praxiteles is still with us. Is it really the same Hermes that it was when it was made? Is its personal identity a fixed state, or does its personality, like our own, change in the passage of time? May it not be the nature of art to cast off what is mortal, and emancipate itself from the mind of its creator? Is it truly immortal, still alive, or only a stone image forever the same—a petrifaction, as it were, of the artist's soul at a certain moment? or is it possible, on the other hand, that such a life really abides in art as to make what is immortal in the work greatly exceed that mortal and temporary part which historical criticism preserves? Let us ignore the historical element, and consider what is left in the critical act, still conceived as a re-creation of the image, but the re-creation of the image before us apart from any attempt to realize what was in the artist's mind, or with only a passing reference to that.

Expression is the nucleus of the artist's power. What is expression? It is the process of externalizing what was in the artist's mind, in some object of sense which shall convey it to others. The material used may be actual form and color, as in painting and sculpture; or imaginary objects and actions through the medium of language, as in literature; or pure sound, as in music: always there is some material which is perceived by the senses and intelligible only through their mediation.

George Edward Woodberry

Slight, indeed, would be the artist's power and inept his skill, if he should not so frame the lineaments of his work as to stamp on the senses of all comers the same intelligible image, and give for the bodily eye what the bodily eye can see in picture, statue or story. The work of art, however, is not merely the material object, but that object charged with the personality of the artist. It is in his power to make that charge effective that his true faculty of expression lies. The material object—form, color, action, sound—is enveloped in his feeling; the words he uses are loaded with his meanings and tones. His personality is immaterial, and cannot be bodied forth; hence, the most essential and significant part of what he expresses, that which clothes the material object with its spirituality, is dependent in a supreme degree on suggestion, on what can be only incompletely set forth, on half-lights and intimations, and the thousand subtleties which lie on the borderland of the inexpressible.

In so far as a work of art is a thing of nature, it can be expressed materially with the more adequacy; in so far as it is a thing of

Two Phases of Criticism

the spirit, of personality, it is less subject to complete and certain expression; and in all art there are these two elements. In that process of re-creating the image which we are now examining, the mind's fortune with these two elements is unequal; so far as the material part is concerned, normal eyes will see the same thing, normal intelligence will grasp the same thing, in figure, action and event; but when it is a question of realizing the spirit, differences begin to emerge and multiply. Rifts of temperament and varieties of experience between artist and spectator make chasms of misunderstanding and misappreciation. How diverse are the representations in the mind finally, as revealed in our tastes and judgments! The same image, mirrored in individuals, becomes radically different in opposed minds, and each is apt to believe that his own is the true and only one. It is a commonplace that every reader thinks that he is Hamlet. What a number of Hamlets that makes! It is a commonplace also that this ease of identification with a character is a test of genius in a writer and ranks him in power and significance.

65

George Edward Woodberry

Those who create so are called the universal writers. Whence arises this paradox, so common in art, of infinite diversity in identity? It comes from the fact that, so far from realizing the image as it was in the artist's mind and receiving it charged with his personality merely, it is we ourselves who create the image by charging it with our own personality. In this creation we do not simply repeat in ourselves his state of mind and become as it were ghosts of him who is dead; but we originate something new, living and our own. There is no other way for us to appropriate his work, to interpret it and understand it. The fact is that a work of art, being once created and expressed, externalized, is gone from the artist's mind and returns to the world of nature; it becomes a part of our external world, and we treat it precisely as we treat the rest of that world, as mere material for our own artist-life which goes on in our own minds and souls in the exercise of our own powers in their limitations. Our appropriation of art is as strictly held within these bounds as is our grasp upon the material world.

It is one of the charms of art that it is not

to be completely understood. In an age in which so high a value is put upon facts, information, positive knowledge, it is a relief to have still reserved to us a place apart where it is not necessary to know all. The truth of science is stated in a formula of mathematics, a law of physics, a generalization of one or another kind; it is clear, and it is all contained there; in each specific case there is nothing more to be known. The truth of art is of a different sort; it does not seem to be all known, finished and finally stated, but on the contrary to be ever growing, more rich in significance, more profound in substance, disclosing heaven over heaven and depth under depth. The greatest books share our lives, and grow old with us; we read them over and over, and at each decade it is a new book that we find there, so much has it gained in meaning from experience of life, from ripening judgment, from the change of seasons in the soul.

A second but powerful limitation lies in those differences of temperament, just referred to, which have an arbitrary potency in appreciation. The practical man is, as a rule, really self-excluded from the field of art; but, inside the field, the stoic will not make much of Byron nor the cynic of Shelley. In certain arts, such as the many kinds of prints, a special training of the eye and some technical knowledge of processes must be acquired before one really sees what the eye itself must discover in the engraving in order to apprehend its subtle qualities. The way, however, is most commonly blocked by certain inhibitions which are so lodged in the mind by education and opinion that they effectively paralyze any effort at re-creation. The prejudice of the early New England church against the theater is a curious instance of an inhibition that rendered nugatory a great historic branch of art, the drama; and it is the more singular, viewed as a religious phenomenon, because of the great place the drama held in religion itself in Catholic countries and especially in medieval times. What Puritan could read the sacred drama of Spain with any understanding? I have friends who object to war as a theme of verse, and the praise of wine by the poets is anathema in many quarters. These are all examples of moral inhibitions bred in the com-

munity and operating against great divisions
of literature. What a sword of destruction
that would be which would strike Mars and
Bacchus from the world's poetry! The American inhibition, however, which best illustrates
what I have in mind, is that which rejects
the nude in sculpture and painting, not only
forfeiting thereby the supreme of Greek genius
and sanity, but to the prejudice, also, of human
dignity, as it seems to me.

Such inhibitions in one way and another
exist in communities and individuals; the appreciation of literature, and of art in general,
is subject to them; and I cite these examples
to bring out clearly how true it is that, almost
involuntarily and unconsciously, in re-creating
the work of art we remake it in ourselves and
not in its own old world, and the meaning
we charge it with is our own personality and
not that of its original creator. If I look with
shamed eyes at Hermes, Narcissus and Venus,
the shame is mine, and not the sculptor's; if
I cannot read the old verses on Agincourt with
sympathy and delight in their heroic breath,
the poverty of soul is mine, not Drayton's.
In every way, the responsibility for what we

make of art, in re-creating it, springs from
what we are.

It is plain that, in consequence of our various limitations in faculty, knowledge, experience, temperament and working always with
some subjection to communal ideas and tastes,
we must suffer many losses of what the work
of art originally contained and fall short of
realizing it as it was in the artist's mind. On
the other hand there is some compensation in
the fact that the work itself may take on new
meanings that the artist did not dream of;
for, in returning to the external world and
becoming a part of our real environment, the
work of art has resumed that plastic quality
which belongs to the world of nature and
makes it material for us to mold our own souls
in. The essence of the work, its living power
for us, is not what the artist put in it, but
what we draw from it; its world-value is not
what it was to the artist, but what it is to the
world. It is common enough for the reader
to find meanings in a book that the writer did
not consciously put there; there is much in personality that the artist himself is not aware
of, and also there may be much in the work

Two Phases of Criticism

which he does not attend to, and hence there is excess of significance in both ways; and moreover, the reader may respond to the work with greater sensitiveness than belonged to the creator and in new ways. Thus arises the paradox which I often maintain, that it is not the poet, but the reader, who writes the poem. . . .

If you have followed these remarks with any sympathy and I have conveyed to you my belief that each of us has the artist-soul, continually engaged in its own creations, you will readily comprehend that works of art are not to me historical monuments valuable for the information they give of the past, nor even artistic entities to be known apart from ourselves and as they were in the artist's mind; but rather such works are only raw material, or at least new material, for us to make our own statues and pictures and poems out of; or, in a word, to create the forms of our own souls out of; for the soul must be given forms in order to be aware of its being, to know itself, truly to be. The soul moves toward self-expression in many ways, but in finding forms for itself the soul discovers its most plastic material in the world of art. It is in forms of ideality that the soul hastens to clothe itself; and while it is possible for us to elaborate such forms from the crude mass of nature, as the first artists did, yet later generations are the more fortunate in that they possess in art and literature a vast treasure of ideality already elaborated and present. Works of art thus constitute a select material wherein the artist-soul that is in each of us can work, not only with our own native force of penetration and aspiration, but, as it were, with higher aid—the aid of genius, the aid of the select souls of the race. . . .

It has become plain, I trust, in what sense it is indeed true that it is the nature of art to cast off what is mortal and emancipate itself from the mind of its creator, and thus to enter upon a life of its own, continually renewed in the minds of those who appropriate it. This is its real immortality—not the fact that it lasts through time, but that it lives in the souls of mankind. I am fond of biography, and few are the pleasures of the literary life that are more pure and precious than the quiet and unknown companionship which biography may establish between ourselves and those whose works have endeared to us their persons and interested us in their human fortunes as if they were friends; but I am always glad when time has destroyed all merely mortal record of them, and there remains only their work—only the "souls of poets dead and gone." . . .

Only that element abides which can enter continuously and permanently into the souls of men, according to their several grades of being—only that which can live in humanity; the rest fades away with time. And then this miracle arises that into the soul of Virgil, for example, enters a Christian soul, new-born, and deepening its pathos; and not Virgil only, but many others, are, as it were, adopted into the race itself and become the ever growing children of the human spirit, ideals and fathers of ideals through ages. That is earthly immortality—the survival and increment of the spirit through time. Thus arises another paradox, that as art begins by being charged with personality, it ends by becoming impersonal, solving the apparent contradiction in the soul universal, the common soul of mankind. Each

of us creates art in his own image—it seems
an infinite variable; and yet it is the variable
of something identical in all—the soul. I
often think that in the artistic life, and its
wonderful spiritual interchange through the
re-creation in each of the ideals of all, there
is realized something analogous to the religious
conception of the communion of saints, especially when one considers the impersonality of
art in its climax of world-fame; for the communion of saints is not a communion of individual with individual, but of each one with
all. It is thus in the artistic life that one
shares in the soul universal, the common soul
of mankind, which yet is manifest only in individuals and their concrete works. Art like
life has its own material being in the concrete,
but the spiritual being of both is in the universal.

We have come, then, in our examination of
criticism, or, in other words, of the act of
appreciation, to the point I indicated earlier
upon opening the subject, where criticism appears to be a private affair, a deeply personal
act, such that every one of us must be his
own artist. Each of us has the artist-soul,

Two Phases of Criticism

and if we enter truly into the world of art, it is not merely as spectators, but as participants, as ourselves the artists. It is on this activity of the soul in its artist-life that the whole subject concentrates its interest. I reminded you that from time to time in history our ancestors encountered successively alien literatures, and as each was in turn appropriated, a Renaissance resulted. It is thus that civilization has grown in body and quality, ever enriching itself by what it absorbs from this and that particular race and age. Nothing can exceed in folly the policy and temper that would isolate nations and races one from another; it is from the intermingling of all, with their various gifts and labors, that the greatest good finally comes; and no sign of the times is so disturbing to me as the present reactionary tendency in America apparent in the growth of race-prejudice and a jealous contempt of the foreigner. In this respect the life of the individual is like that of nations. If he grows, it is often by a Renaissance attending the introduction of something novel into his life. You are all familiar with the splendid burst of the human spirit which at-

tended the re-discovery of the ancient classic
world in Italy, and you will recall how at a
later time the re-discovery of the Middle Ages
occasioned a similar flowering of art in the
Gothic Renaissance, so variously fruitful in
its turn in the last century. The parallel is
easily found in individual life; such a profound and developing experience was the Italian journey for Goethe, the study of Plato and
the Greek dramatists for Shelley, mythology
for Keats—and everywhere in literary biography one finds illustrations.

The most arresting trait of the artist-life,
as one begins to lead it, is that it is a life of
discovery. It is not truth that is discovered,
but faculty; what results is not an acquisition
of knowledge, but an exercise of inward power.
The most wonderful thing in the soul is the
extraordinary latency of power in it; and it is
in the artist-life, in the world of art, that this
latent power is most variously and brilliantly
released. What happens to you when you begin to see, really to see, pictures, for example?
It is not that a new object has come within
the range of your vision; but that a new power
of seeing has arisen in your eye, and through

Two Phases of Criticism

this power a new world has opened before you
—a world of such marvels of space, color and
beauty, luminosity, shadow and line, atmosphere and disposition, that you begin to live
in it as a child begins to learn to live in the
natural world. It is not the old world seen
piece-meal; it is a new world on another level
of being than natural existence. So, when
you begin to take in a poem, it is not a mere
fanciful arrangement of idea and event added
to your ordinary memory of things; new
powers of feeling have opened in your heart
that constitute a fresh passion of life there,
and as you feel it with lyric and drama, a
significance, a mystery, a light enter into the
universe as you know it, with transforming
and exalting power. It is not that you have
acquired knowledge; you have acquired heart.
To lead the artist-life is not to look at pictures and read books; it is to discover the
faculties of the soul, that slept unknown and
unused, and to apply them in realizing the
depth and tenderness, the eloquence, the hope
and joy, of the life that is within. It is by
this that the life of art differs from the life
of science: its end is not to know, but to be.

George Edward Woodberry

The revolt against the historical treatment of art arises from feeling that in such treatment art loses its own nature, and that what is truly life, and has its only value as life, is degraded into what is merely knowledge. The first place is held by life. It is against the substitution of knowledge for life in scholarship, especially in the literary and artistic fields, that the protest is made.

A second main trait of the artist-life of the soul, for which I am, as it were, pleading, is that it is a life of growth by an inward secret and mysterious process. There is nothing mechanical in it; it is vital. It was this aspect of the soul's life which Wordsworth brought so prominently forward, and made elemental in his verse, advocating a "wise passiveness" in the conduct of the mind:

> "Think you, 'mid all this mighty sum
> Of things forever speaking,
> That nothing of itself will come,
> But we must still be seeking?"

"Consider the lilies, how they grow: they toil not, neither do they spin." That is the type of the artist-soul; in the artist-life there is neither toiling nor spinning. In an economical

Two Phases of Criticism

civilization like ours, leisure is apt to be confounded with indolence, and it is hard to see
how the poet watching

> "the sun illume
> The yellow bees in the ivy bloom,"

is not an idler in the land. Especially is it
hard to see how things will come without planning. In our own day planning has become
an all-engrossing occupation. A belief in organization has spread through the country, and
is applied in all quarters of life, as if success
were always a matter of machinery, and preferably of legislative machinery. . . . There is
a part of life where planning, the adjustment
of means to an end, organization, and all that
belongs in the practical sphere, has its place;
but the growth of the soul proceeds on other
principles and in another realm. The artist-
life of the soul—and the soul's life is characteristically artistic—lies in the self-revelation
of its own nature, and this is a growth which
takes place in a world of beauty, passion, adoration—in a word, of ideality, where what
Wordsworth calls "our meddling intellect,"
the practical reason, has small part.

George Edward Woodberry

I well know how opposed this doctrine is to the ruling spirit of our time, which shrinks our lives to the limits of an economical and mechanical sphere, to use Eucken's phrases, and accustoms us to the dominance of their precepts and methods. Art with difficulty finds room among us. It is not by accident that our most literary temperament, Henry James, and our two great artists, Whistler and Sargent, have had their homes abroad, and that from the beginning the literature and art of America have often had their true locality on a foreign soil. Yet, whatever may be the seeming, it is always true that the soul grows, it is not made; and the world of art is chiefly precious to us because it is a place for the soul's growth.

A third main trait of the world of art is that it is a place of freedom. I have already alluded to this briefly. It is not merely that the soul is there freed from the manacles of utility and has escaped from the great burden of success in life; that is only the negative side. It has also, on the positive side, entered into a realm of new power, the exercise of which is its highest function. The soul tran-

Two Phases of Criticism

scends nature, and reconstitutes the world in the image of its own finer vision and deeper wisdom, realizing ideality in its own consciousness and conveying at least the shadow of its dream to mankind. It transcends nature in creating form. The Hermes of Praxiteles, whether or not one knows it is Hermes and discerns in it the godlike nature, gives to all ages a figure such as nature never shaped. The soul, also, in its artist-life, transcends nature in idea; each of us, in reading the play, may believe he is Hamlet, but each is well aware that he is identifying himself with a more perfect type of himself, such as is known only to the mind's eye. And, similarly, the soul transcends nature in the field of the relations of things; it builds up an Arcadia, an earthly Paradise, an ideal state, a forest of Arden, an island-kingdom of Prospero, a Round Table, a School of Athens, a Last Judgment, a legend of the Venusberg—what not?—so vast and various is the imaginary world wherein the soul from the beginning has bodied forth that inner vision and wisdom in which it finds its true self-consciousness. So great is its freedom there that, as is often said, it transcends also

the moral world, and so far as morals belong
in the sphere of mere utility and social arrangement, this must be granted; but the subject is too large and complicated to be entered
upon here. I allude to it only to emphasize
and bring out fully the doctrine that the soul
exercises in its artist-life an unchartered freedom; for it is not concerned there with practical results of any kind, but only with the
discovery of its nature, both active and passive.

The fruit of this large freedom is the ideal
world, in which each realizes his dream of the
best. It is here that experiments are made,
that revolutions sometimes begin; for the ideal,
as I have said, once expressed, passes back
into the ordinary world, and there it may be
made a pattern, a thing to be actualized, and
it falls under the dominance of the practical
reason and has this or that fortune according
to the wisdom or folly of mankind at the time.
The ideal world is very mutable in different
ages and races; and history is full of its débris.
It is not an everlasting city set in the heavens
that shall some time descend upon the earth
in a millennium; it is a dream, the dream of

Two Phases of Criticism

the soul in its creative response to the world about it. Yet there is nothing insubstantial about the dream; however unrealized in the external world of fact, it is spiritually real, for it is lived in the soul—it is the conscious life of the soul. There are times, however, when the ideal world does enter into the actual world, and partly permeate it, if it does not wholly master it. The classic, the chivalric, the Christian world attest the fact, broadly; and in individual life how must we ourselves bear witness to the mingling in ourselves of the poet's blood—which is the blood of the world. In the intimacy of this communion is our best of life, and it is accomplished solely by the re-creation in us, in our minds and hearts, our hopes, admirations and loves, of what was first in the artists of every sort, according to our capacity to receive and re-embody in our own spiritual substance their finer, wiser, deeper power. Their capacity to enter thus into the life of humanity is the measure of their genius, and our capacity to receive the gift is the measure of our souls.

Such in its main lines is the artist-life of the soul, a life of discovery, of growth, of freedom; but what is most precious in it, and most characterizes it, is a prophetic quality that abides in its experiences. The poets are often spoken of as prophets, and in history the greatest are those most lonely peaks that seem to have taken the light of an unrisen dawn, like Virgil, whose humanity in the "Æneid" shines with a foregleam of the Christian temperament, or like Plato, whose philosophy in many a passage was a morning star that went before the greater light of Christian faith in the divine. But it is not such poets and such prophecy that I have in mind. I mean that in our own experiences in this artist-life with the poets, sculptors and musicians there abides the feeling that we shall have, as Tennyson says, "the wages of going on"—there is our clearest intimation of immortality. Wordsworth found such intimations in fragments of his boyhood and youth. I find them rather in fragments of manhood and maturer life. Life impresses me less as a birth initially out of the divine into mortal being than as birth into the divine at each step of the onward way. I am always fearful that in such statements, and in such a discourse as

this has been, I may seem to be speaking of
exceptional things, of life that is only for the
select and methods that are practicable only
for the few and for men especially endowed
with rare temperaments. Nothing could be
further from my own belief. The artist-life
of the soul is common to all, as soon as the
soul begins to be and breathe, for it is in the
world of art that the soul lives. The boy
with Homer, the sage with Plato—it is all
one: each is finding his soul, and living in it.
The herb of grace grows everywhere.

I have never such firm conviction of the
divine meaning that abides in our life as when
I notice how the soul puts forth its flower in
the humblest lives and in the most neglected
places, what deeds of the spirit are simply
done by the poor and almost as if they did
not know it. It is true that human life is an
animal existence, and the sphere of the useful
is primary in it; the necessity for earning one's
food, building one's lodging, caring for one's
offspring, governs our days and years; but if
I am in favor of social betterment and a
more just economic order in the state to lessen
the burden of common life and free it from

an animal enslavement, it is not that I am
thinking so much of what is called the welfare
of the masses, in the sense of comfort. It is
because I desire for them the leisure which
would leave their souls room to grow. I
should be sorry to see material comfort, which
is an animal good, become the ideal of the
state, as now seems the tendency. We are all
proud of America, and look on our farms and
workshops, the abundance of work, the harvest
of universal gain dispersed through multitudes
reclaimed from centuries of poverty—we see
and proclaim the greatness of the good; but
I am ill-content with the spiritual harvest,
with the absence of that which has been the
glory of great nations in art and letters, with
the indifference to that principle of human
brotherhood in devotion to which our fathers
found greatness and which is most luminous
in art and letters; our enormous success in the
economical and mechanical sphere leaves me
unreconciled to our failure to enter the artistic
sphere as a nation.

There is always, however, as you know, "a
remnant." It is true that the conditions of
our time almost enforce upon our citizens, es-

pecially as they grow old and become absorbed in the work of the world, so abundant and compelling here—it is true that these conditions almost enforce a narrowly practical life. But there is one period of life when this pressure is less felt, and when nature herself seems to open the gateways for this artist-life that I have been speaking of: it is youth. I hope some random sentence, perhaps, may have made it easier for some one of you who are young, to believe in that world, to follow its beckoning lights and to lead its life.

Criticism [1]

By w. c. BROWNELL

I. *Field and Function*

CRITICISM itself is much criticized—which logically establishes its title. No form of mental
activity is commoner, and, where the practice
of anything is all but universal, protest against
it is as idle as apology for it should be superfluous. The essentially critical character of form-
ularies alleging the inferiority to books of
the books about books that Lamb preferred,
finding the genesis of criticism in creative failure, and so on, should of itself demonstrate
that whatever objection may be made to it in
practice there can be none in theory. In which
case the only sensible view is that its practice
should be perfected rather than abandoned.
However, it is probably only in—may one say?

---

[1] From a volume entitled *Criticism*, published by Charles
Scribner's Sons in 1914. Of the four chapters in that volume, on "Field and Function," "Equipment," "Criterion,"
and "Method," the first and the last are here reprinted by
permission of the publishers.

88

Criticism

—"uncritical circles," notoriously as sceptical about logic as about criticism, that it encounters this fundamental censure. "Nobody here," Lord Morley remarked, addressing the English Association, "will undervalue criticism or fall into the gross blunder of regarding it as a mere parasite of creative work." And, indeed, it would be slighting just proportion and intellectual decorum to lay any particular stress on the aspersions of the sprightly sciolists of the studios, such as, for example, the late Mr. Whistler, and of brilliant literary adventurers, such as, for another instance, the late Lord Beaconsfield.

As a matter of fact these two rather celebrated disparagers of criticism were greatly indebted to the critical faculty, very marked in each of them. It is now becoming quite generally appreciated, I imagine,—thanks to criticism,—that Degas's admonition to Whistler about his conduct cheapening his talent, which every one will remember, embodied a slight misconception. Whistler's achievements in painting, however incontestable their merits, would certainly have enjoyed less of the vogue he so greatly prized had his prescription that work should be "received in silence" been followed in his own case by himself. And it was certainly the critical rather than the creative element in Disraeli's more serious substance that gave it the interest it had for his contemporaries, and has now altogether lost.

More worth while recalling than Disraeli's inconsistency, however, is the fact that in plagiarizing he distorted Coleridge's remark, substituting "critics" for "reviewers" as those who had failed in creative fields. The substitution is venial in so far as in the England of that day the critics were the reviewers. But this is what is especially noteworthy in considering the whole subject: namely, that in England, as with ourselves, the art of criticism is so largely the business of reviewing as to make the two, in popular estimation at least, interconvertible terms. They order the matter differently in France. Every one must have been struck at first by the comparative slightness of the reviewing in French journalism. One's impression at first is that they take the business much less seriously than one would expect in a country with such an active interest

Criticism

in art and letters. The papers, even the reviews, concern themselves with the current product chiefly in the "notice" or the *compte rendu*, which aims merely to inform the reader as to the contents of the book or the contributions to the exposition, whatever it may be, with but a meager addition of comment either courteous or curt. The current art criticism even of Gautier, even of Diderot for that matter, is largely descriptive. In the literary *revues* what we should call the reviewing is apt to be consigned to a few back pages of running *chronique*, or a supplementary leaflet.

Of course one explanation is that the French public reads and sees for itself too generally to need or savor extensive treatment of the essentially undifferentiated. The practice of reviewing scrupulously all the output of the novel factories, exemplified by such periodicals as even the admirable *Athenæum*, would seem singular to it. But with us, even when the literature reviewed is eminent and serious, it is estimated, when it is reviewed with competence, by the anonymous expert, who confines himself to the matter in hand and delivers a kind of bench decision in a circumscribed case.

And in France this is left to subsequent books or more general articles, with the result of releasing the critic for more personal work of larger scope. Hence, there are a score of French critics of personal quality for one English or American. Even current criticism becomes a province of literature instead of being a department of routine. Our own current criticism, anonymous or other, is, I need not say, largely of this routine character, when it has character, varied by the specific expert decision in a very few quarters, and only occasionally by a magazine *article de fond* of a real synthetic value. This last I should myself like to see the Academy, whose function must be mainly critical, encourage by every means open to it, by way of giving more *standing* to our criticism, which is what I think it needs first of all.

For the antipathy to criticism I imagine springs largely from confounding it with the reviewing—which I do not desire to depreciate, but to distinguish from criticism of a more personal order and a more permanent appeal. The tradition of English reviewing is impressive, and it is natural that Coleridge should

Criticism

have spoken of reviewers as a class, and that
Mr. Birrell should have them exclusively in
mind in defining the traits of the ideal critic.
And we ourselves are not without journals
which review with obvious resources of scholarship and skill, and deliver judgments with the
tone, if not always with the effect, of finality.
But of course, taking the country as a whole,
reviewing is the least serious concern of the
journalism that seems to take so many things
lightly. And it is this reviewing that I fancy
the authors and artists have in mind when
they disparage criticism. They disparage it
in the main, however, as insufficiently expert,
but though I dare say this is often just, the
objection to it which is apparently not considered, but which I should think even more
considerable, is its tendency to monopolize the
critical field and establish this very ideal of
specific expertness, which its practice so frequently fails to realize, as the ideal of criticism in general. This involves, I think, a
restricted view of the true critic's field, and
an erroneous view of his function. Virtually
it confines his own field to that of the practice
he criticizes; and his function to that of esti-

mating any practice with reference to its technical standards. In a word, expert criticism is necessarily technical criticism, and, not illogically, those whose ideal it is insist that the practitioner himself is the only proper critic of his order of practice.

This was eminently the view of the late Russell Sturgis, who had an inexhaustible interest in technic of all kinds and maintained stoutly that only artists should write about art. And though his own practice negatived his principle so far as painting and sculpture are concerned, that was perhaps because the painters and sculptors were themselves so remiss in lending a hand to the work he deemed it important to have done. They were surely excusable, in many cases, since they could allege preoccupation with what they could do even better, in proportion as they were either satisfactorily good at it or successful with it. Sturgis's theory was that art should be interpreted from the artist's point of view, assuming of course the existence of such a point of view. As a matter of fact there is none, and when it is sought what is found is either *an* artist's point of view, which is personal and

not professional, or else it is that of every one
else sufficiently educated in the results which
artists could hardly have produced for centuries without, sooner or later, at least betray-
ing what it is their definite aim distinctly to
express. The esoteric in their work is a matter, not of art,—the universal language in
which they communicate,—but of science; it
does not reside in the point of view, but in
the process.

All artistic accomplishment divides itself
naturally, easily, and satisfactorily, however
loosely, into the two categories, moral and
material. The two certainly overlap, and this
is particularly true of the plastic arts, whose
peculiarity—or whose distinction, if you choose
—is to appeal to the senses as well as to the
mind. A certain technic therefore—that is
to say, the science of their material side—
is always to be borne in mind. But a far less
elaborate acquaintance with this than is vital
to the practitioner is ample for the critic, who
may in fact easily have too much of it if he
have any inclination to exploit rather than
to subordinate it. He may quite conceivably
profit by Arnold's caution: "To handle these

matters properly, there is needed a poise so perfect that the least overweight in any direction tends to destroy the balance . . . even erudition may destroy it. Little as I know therefore, I am always apprehensive, in dealing with poetry, lest even that little should [quoting a remark by the Duke of Wellington] 'prove too much for my abilities.' "

The artist who exacts more technical expertness from the critic than he finds is frequently looking in criticism for what it is the province of the studio to provide; he requires of it the educational character proper to the classroom, or the qualifications pertinent to the hanging committee. Now, even confined within its proper limits, this esoteric criticism suffers from its inherent concentration on technic. Artistic innovation meets nowhere with such illiberal hostility as it encounters in its own hierarchy, and less on temperamental than on technical grounds. On the other hand, a painter like Bouguereau may systematically invert the true relations of conception and execution, employing the most insipid conventionalities to express his exquisite drawing, and remain for a generation the head of the pro-

fessional corner in a school edifice where the
critical faculty seems sometimes paralyzed by
the technical criterion. And of course in technical circles such a criterion tends to establish
itself. Millet, who refused to write about a
fellow painter's work for the precise reason
that he was a painter himself and therefore
partial to his own different way of handling
the subject, was a practitioner of exceptional
breadth of view, and would perhaps have
agreed with Aristotle, who, as Montaigne says,
"will still have a hand in everything," and
who asserts that the proper judge of the tiller
is not the carpenter but the helmsman. Indeed, "The wearer knows where the shoe
pinches" is as sound a maxim as *"Ne sutor
ultra crepidam";* and the authority of the latter itself may be invoked in favor of leaving
criticism to critics. The classics of esthetic
criticism constitute an impressive body of literature, which has been of immense interpre-
tative service to art, and to which the only
practicing contributor of signal importance, it
is worth bearing in mind, was himself a lit-
térateur—even a novelist and a poet. Nor
does it seem singular that, as a rule and in pro-

portion to his seriousness, the practitioner should be engrossed by practice.

It is true that we have in America—possibly in virtue of our inevitable eclecticism—a considerable number of practicing artists who also write distinguished criticism. But to ascribe its excellence to their technical expertness, rather than to their critical faculty and literary ability, would really be doing an injustice to the felicity with which they subordinate in their criticism all technical parade beyond that which is certainly too elementary to be considered esoteric. Certainly some of them would be indisposed to measure work by their own practice, and in that case what critical title does this practice in itself confer? As a rule indeed, I think, they rather help than hinder the contention that criticism is a special province of literature with, in fact, a technic of its own in which they show real expertness, instead of a literary adjunct of the special art with which it is variously called upon to concern itself. And in this special province, material data are far less considerable than moral—with which latter, accordingly, it is the special function of criticism to deal. Every one is familiar with plastic works of a perfection that all the technical talk in the world would not explain, as no amount of technical expertness could compass it. However young the artist might have begun to draw, or model, or design, whatever masters he might have had, however long he might have practiced his art, whatever his skill, native or acquired, whatever his professional expertness, in a word, no artist could have achieved the particular result in question without those *qualities* which have controlled the result, and which it is the function of criticism to signalize, as it is the weakness of expert evaluation to neglect.

Criticism, thus, may not inexactly be described as the statement of the concrete in terms of the abstract. It is its function to discern and characterize the abstract qualities informing the concrete expression of the artist. Every important piece of literature, as every important work of plastic art, is the expression of a personality, and it is not the material of it, but the mind behind it, that invites critical interpretation. Materially speaking, it is its own interpretation. The concrete absorbs the constructive artist whose endeavor is to give substance to his idea, which until expressed is an abstraction. The concern of criticism is to measure his success by the correspondence of his expression to the idea it suggests and by the value of the idea itself. The critic's own language, therefore, into which he is to translate the concrete work he is considering, is the language of the abstract; and as in translation what is needed is appreciation of the foreign tongue and expertness in one's own, it is this language that it behooves him especially to cultivate.

As it is the *qualities* of the writer, painter, sculptor, and not the *properties* of their productions, that are his central concern, as his function is to disengage the moral value from its material expression,—I do not mean of course in merely major matters, but in minutiæ as well, such as even the lilt of a verse or the drawing of a wrist, the distinction being one of kind, not of rank,—qualities, not properties, are the very substance and not merely the subject of the critic's own expression. The true objects of his contemplation are the multifarious elements of truth, beauty,

Criticism

goodness, and their approximations and antipodes, underlying the various phenomena which express them, rather than the laws and rules peculiar to each form of phenomenal expression; which, beyond acquiring the familiarity needful for adequate appreciation, he may leave to the professional didacticism of each. And in thus confining itself to the art and eschewing the science of whatever forms its subject—mindful mainly of no science, indeed, except its own—criticism is enabled to extend its field while restricting its function, and to form a distinct province of literature, while relinquishing encroachments upon the territory of more exclusively constructive art.

Of course thus individualizing the field and the function of criticism neither predicates universal capacity in nor prescribes universal practice to the individual critic, who however will specialize all the more usefully for realizing that both his field and his function are themselves as special as his faculty is universally acknowledged to be.

W. C. Brownell

II. *Method*

A rational criterion implies a constructive
method. In itself analysis reaches no conclusion, which is the end and aim of reason. Invaluable as is its service in detail, some rational
ideal must underlie its processes, and if these
are to be fruitful they must determine the relations of the matter in hand to this ideal,
and even in dissection contribute to the synthesis that constitutes the essence of every work
of any individuality. The weak joint in
Sainte-Beuve's armor is his occasional tendency
to rest in his analysis. It is the finer art to suggest the conclusion rather than to draw it, no
doubt, but one should at least do that; and
I think Sainte-Beuve, in spite of his search for
the *faculté maîtresse* and his anticipation of
the race, the *milieu*, and the moment theory
so hard worked by Taine, occasionally fails to
justify his analysis in this way; so that his
result is both artistically and philosophically
inconclusive. Now and then he pays in this
way for his aversion to pedantry and system,
and the excessive disinterestedness of his curiosity.

Criticism

It would certainly be pedantry to insist on truly constructive criticism in every *causerie du lundi* in which a great critic may quite pardonably vary his more important work with the play for which he has a *penchant*. But on the other hand truly constructive criticism does not of necessity involve rigidity. It implies not a system, but a method—to employ the distinction with which Taine defended his procedure, but which assuredly he more or less conspicuously failed to observe. It prescribes, in every work of criticism, a certain independence of its subject, and imposes on it the same constructive obligations that it in turn requires of its theme. A work of criticism is in fact as much a thesis as its theme, and the same thematic treatment is to be exacted of it. And considered in this way as a thesis, its unity is to be secured only by the development in detail of some central conception preliminarily established and constantly referred to, however arrived at, whether by intuition or analysis. The detail thus treated becomes truly contributive and constructive in a way open to no other method. We may say indeed that all criticism of moment, even impressionist criticism, has this synthetic aspect at least, as otherwise it must lack even the appearance of that organic quality necessary to effectiveness. And when we read some very interesting and distinguished criticism—such as the agglutinate and amorphous essays of Lowell, for example—and compare it with concentric and constructive work,—such as *par excellence* that of Arnold,—we can readily see that its failure in force is one of method as well as of faculty.

On the other hand, the constructive method is peculiarly liable to excess. If the central conception it is concerned with is followed out in detail without the checks and rectifications of analysis—the great verifying process —we have the partisanship of Carlyle, the inelasticity of Taine, the prescriptive formulary of Brunetière. The spirit of system stifles freedom of perception and distorts detail. Criticism becomes theoretic. And though theoretic criticism may be, and in fact is not unlikely to be, artistically effective, it is fatally untrustworthy, because it is bent on illustrating its theory in its analysis, instead of merely verifying such features of its cen-

Criticism

tral conception as analysis will confirm. Against such intuitive extravagance as Carlyle's the advantages of remarkable insight may fairly be set off. The academic prescriptions of Brunetière, too, have a distinct educational value—the results of a high-class literary scholiast are always technically instructive, however lacking they may be in the freedom and impressionability sanctioned by a criterion less rigid for being purely rational, and committed to no body of doctrine, traditional or other.

It is, however, the historical method of criticism that chiefly illustrates constructive excess. This method has at present probably the center of the stage; and though there is in France a distinct reaction from the supremacy of Taine and in favor of Sainte-Beuve's sinuous plasticity, the method itself maintains its authority. Taine was an historian and a philosopher rather than a critic, and his criticism is accordingly not so much criticism illuminated by history and philosophy as philosophic history. The data of literature and art under his hand become the "documents" of history, of which in a scientific age

105

we hear so much. His thesis once established, however, as historical rather than literary or esthetic, too much I think can hardly be said for his treatment. Classification has the advantage of clearing up confusion, and the value of a work like the *History of English Literature* appears when one recognizes its paramount merit as resident in the larger scope and general view of history in which of necessity purely individual traits are to some extent blurred if not distorted. These indeed may very well be left to pure criticism whose precise business they are. But the historic method in pure criticism is held quite independently of Taine's authority. Scherer, for example, arguing against "personal sensations" in criticism, maintains that from the study of a writer's character and of his period the right understanding of his work issues spontaneously. This is excellent prescription for the impressionist, although Scherer doubtless means by "personal sensations," personal *judgment* also, and thus minimizes or indeed obliterates perhaps the most essential element of all in criticism, the critic's own personality. Scherer's practice, precisely owing to his personality, far

Criticism

excelled his theory, as to which Arnold reminded him of Macaulay, who certainly knew
his writers and their period, but in whose mind
a right understanding of their works occasionally failed spontaneously to issue.

In fine, the historic method, great as have
been its services to criticism and truly constructive as it is, has two erroneous tendencies.
It tends generally to impose its historical theory on the literary and esthetic facts, to discern their historical rather than their essential
character; and, as inelastically applied, at all
events, it tends specifically to accept its "documents" as final rather than as the very *subjects* of its concern. Taine furnishes a striking instance of the latter practice. I have
never myself been able to agree with those of
his opponents, who, like Brunetière, rested in
the comfortable assurance that his whole theory was overthrown by the fact that the ordinary Venetian gondolier of the period was the
product of the influences that also produced
Tintoretto. One might as well hold that im-
munity in some cases is not the result of the
vaccine that fails to take in others; the causes
of such differences in either physiology or his-

W. C. Brownell

tory being perhaps, so far as they are not obvious, too obscure for profitable discussion compared with the causes of resemblances. But from the critical point of view it *is* a legitimate objection to his rigorous application of his method that he is led by it to consider so disproportionately *causes*, which are the proper subject of history, rather than *characteristics*, which are the true subject of criticism; to deem the business finished, so to say, when it is explained, and, comparatively speaking, to eschew its estimation.

As to the other tendency, that of imposing historical theory on critical data, it is a commonplace that history itself, which has been luminously called philosophy teaching by examples, sometimes suffers from the submergence of its examples by its philosophy. In criticism the result is more serious because, viewed in the same light, its "examples" have a far more salient importance. They are themselves differentiated philosophically in a high degree, and it is correspondingly difficult successfully to treat them merely as pieces of some vaster mosaic. On large lines and in an elementary way, this may of course be use-

fully done, but the work belongs in general
I think rather to the class-room than to the
forum of criticism. In the latter place their
traits call for a treatment at once more individually searching and more conformed to an
abstract, ideal, independent, and rational
standard—for the application to the data they
furnish of the *ideas* they suggest, not the theory they fit.

Now, in the true critical field of independent judgment, however enlightened by culture
and fortified by philosophic training, we know
very well that theory means preconception.
And, carried into any detail of prescription,
preconception is as a matter of fact constantly
being confuted by performance. Divorced
from the ideas proper to each performance,
reposing on a formula derived in its turn from
previous performance become accepted and
consecrate, it is continually disconcerted. New
schools with new formulæ arise as if by some
inherent law, precisely at the apogee of old
ones. And preconception, based as it perforce
is upon some former crystallization of the
diverse and undulating elements of artistic expression, is logically inapplicable at any given

time—*except* as it draws its authority from examples of permanent value and enduring appeal, in which case no one would think of calling it preconception at all. It may be said, to be sure, that philosophically this view, in excluding theory, degrades criticism to an altogether ancillary station—the business of merely furnishing data for an historical synthesis. But I am disinclined to accept this implication until the possibility of an historical synthesis at all comparable in exactness with the critical determination of the data for it is realized or shown to be realizable. The monument that Sainte-Beuve's critical essays constitute is, in spite of their disproportionate analysis, far otherwise considerable than the fascinating historical and evolutionary framework within which Taine's brilliant synthesis so hypnotizes our critical faculty.

In general effect, moreover, Sainte-Beuve's work is itself markedly synthetic. What a complete picture it presents, at the same time continually illustrating the truth that the wiser business of criticism is to occupy itself with examples and the ideas they evoke, not with theories and the systems they threaten! For with examples we have the essential element of unity "given"; it is actual, not problematical. And—impersonal theses of course aside —in criticism of the larger kind as distinct from mere reviewing or expert commentary, by examples we mean, practically, personalities. That is to say, not *Manfred*, but Byron, not the Choral Symphony, but Beethoven. I mean, naturally, so far as personality is expressed in work, and do not suggest invasion of the field of biography except to tact commensurable with that which so notably served Sainte-Beuve. There is here ample scope for the freest exercise of the synthetic method. For personality is the most concrete and consistent entity imaginable, mysteriously unifying the most varied and complicated attributes. The solution of this mystery is the end of critical research. To state it is the crown of critical achievement. The critic may well disembarrass himself of theoretical apparatus, augment and mobilize his stock of ideas, sharpen his faculties of penetration, and set in order all his constructive capacity, before attacking such a complex as any personality, worthy of attention at all, presents at

111

the very outset. If he takes to pieces and puts together again the elements of its composition, and in the process or in the result conveys a correct judgment as well as portrait of the original thus interpreted, he has accomplished the essentially critical part of a task demanding the exercise of all his powers.

And I think he will achieve the most useful result in following the line I have endeavored to trace in the work of the true masters of this branch of literature, the born critics whose practice shows it to be a distinctive branch of literature, having a function, an equipment, a criterion, and a method of its own. This practice involves, let me recapitulate, the initial establishment of some central conception of the subject, gained from specific study illuminated by a general culture, followed by an analysis of detail confirming or modifying this, and concluding with a synthetic presentation of a physiognomy whose features are as distinct as the whole they compose—the whole process interpenetrated by an estimate of value based on the standard of reason, judging the subject freely after the laws of the latter's own projection, and not

Criticism

by its responsiveness to either individual whim or formulated prescription. This, at all events, is the ideal illustrated, with more or less closeness, by not only such critics as Sainte-Beuve, Scherer, and Arnold, but such straightforward apostles of pure good sense as Sarcey and Émile Faguet.

How the critic conducts his criticism will of course depend upon his own personality, and the ranks of criticism contain perhaps as great a variety of types and individuals as is to be found in any other field of artistic expression. For, beyond denial, criticism is itself an art; and, as many of its most successful products have been entitled "portraits," sustains a closer analogy at its best with plastic portraiture than with such pursuits as history and philosophy, which seek system through science. One of Sainte-Beuve's studies is as definitely a portrait as one of Holbein's; and on the other hand a portrait by Sargent, for example, is only more obviously and not more really a critical product than are the famous "portraits" that have interpreted to us the generations of the great. More exclusively imaginative art the critic must, it is true, forego.

W. C. Brownell

He would wisely, as I have contended, confine himself to portraiture and eschew the panorama. In essaying a "School of Athens" he is apt, rather, to produce a "Victory of Constantine." His direct aim is truth even in dealing with beauty, forgetting which his criticism is menaced with transmutation into the kind of poetry that one "drops into" rather than attains.

I have dwelt on the esthetic as well as the literary field in the province of criticism, and insisted on the esthetic element as well as the historic in the culture that criticism calls for, because in a very true and fundamental sense art and letters are one. They are so at all events in so far as the function of criticism is concerned, and dictate to this the same practice. Current philosophy may find a pragmatic sanction for a pluralistic universe, but in the criticism of art, whether plastic or literary, we are all "monists." The end of our effort is a true estimate of the data encountered in the search for that beauty which from Plato to Keats has been virtually identified with truth, and the highest service of criticism is to secure that the true and the beautiful, and not the ugly and the false, may in wider and wider circles of appreciation be esteemed to be the good.

The Critics and Young America [1]

By VAN WYCK BROOKS

In that very interesting testament, *Literature in Ireland*, which he left for his fellow-poets, Thomas MacDonagh showed how disadvantageous it is to have a full-grown criticism side by side with what he calls a baby literature. "There is," he says, "a school of criticism in Ireland, a school that knows the work of the finest critics in the world, and knows too, what is more important, the finest literature in the world. This, when dealing with literature in general, adds to the store of fine critical work. This at times encourages and approves good original Irish work. I think it unfortunate, however, that it should have grown with, or indeed before, the original work. Dealing with the monuments of the older literatures—English, French, and the like—this criticism knows

[1] Originally published in 1917 in *The Seven Arts;* reprinted in 1918 in *Letters and Leadership;* and here reprinted (as revised by the author for this collection) by permission of the publishers, B. W. Huebsch, Inc.

116

its place, its bearings, its conditions. Dealing with a naissant literature it looks over its shoulder, as it were. Its neck is awry. Its eyes are twisted round. Its feet turn from their known way and stumble. When it does get a clear view of its object, it misses the shapes and forms it saw in other lands and expresses its disappointment."

Of our own criticism, of our own critics, one could hardly have a better description than that. For Ireland and America really are alike in that they inherit a dominant academic tradition colonial in essence, having its home in centres of civilization remote from the springs of a national life which has only of late come into its own consciousness. In a famous essay Matthew Arnold said that it is "the business of the critical power to see the object as in itself it really is"; for by doing so it "tends to make an intellectual situation of which the creative power can profitably avail itself." There, surely, is the very thing that Young America needs; for what is the power without the situation? Our critics have not made that situation: is it not because they have failed to see the "object"? They have not observed

the groping creative life of America; they have
not observed the conditions that hamper and
enfeeble it. Consequently, they have not been
able to stimulate and focus it—with the result
that it remains a "baby literature" indeed.

I

It is all too evident, in fact, in the America
of to-day that our inherited culture—the culture of which our critics are the spokesmen—
has utterly failed to meet the exigencies of
our life, to seize and fertilize its roots. It
is extraordinary how that fabric of ideas and
assumptions, of sentiments and memories and
attitudes which made up the civilization of
our fathers has melted away like snow un-
covering the sordid facts of a society that
seems to us now so little advanced on the
path of spiritual evolution. The older generation does not recognize its offspring in the
crude chaotic manifestations of the present
day, but I wonder if it ever considers this universal lapse from grace in the light of cause
and effect? I wonder if it ever suspects that
there must have been some inherent weakness

in a culture that has so lost control of a really
well-disposed younger generation, a culture
which, after being dominant for so long, has
left in its wake a society so little civilized?
What is the secret of its decay? And how
does it happen that we, whose minds are gradually opening to so many living influences of
the past, feel as it were the chill of the grave
as we look back over the spiritual history of
our own race?

It was the culture of an age of pioneering,
the reflex of the spirit of material enterprise
—that is the obvious fact; and with the gradual decay of the impulse of enterprise it has
itself disintegrated like a mummy at the touch
of sunlight. Why? Because it was never a
living, active culture, releasing the creative
energies of men. Its function was rather to
divert these energies, to prevent the anarchical,
sceptical, extravagant, dynamic forces of the
spirit from taking the wind out of the myth
of "progress," that myth imposed by destiny
upon the imagination of our forebears in order
that a great uncharted continent might be subdued to the service of the race.

For the creative impulses of men are always

at war with their possessive impulses, and poetry, as we know, springs from brooding on just those aspects of experience that most retard the swift advance of the acquisitive mind. The spirit of a living culture, which ever has within it some of the acid of Pascal's phrase: "Cæsar was too old to go about conquering the world; he ought to have been more mature"— how could this ever have been permitted to grow up, even supposing that it might have been able to grow up, in a people confronted with forests and prairies and impelled by the necessities of the race to keep their hearts whole and their minds on their task? No, it was essential that everything in men should be repressed and denied that would have slackened their manual energy and made their ingenuity a thing of naught, that would have put questions into their minds, that would have made them static materially and dynamic spiritually, that would have led them to feel too much the disparity between the inherited civilization they had left behind and the environment in which they had placed themselves, that would have neutralized the allure of the exterior ambition which led them on.

The Critics and Young America

Puritanism was a complete philosophy for the pioneer and by making human nature contemptible and putting to shame the charms of life it unleashed the acquisitive instincts of men, disembarrassing those instincts by creating the belief that the life of the spirit is altogether a secret life and that the imagination ought never to conflict with the law of the tribe. It was this that determined the character of our old culture, which cleared the decks for practical action by draining away all the irreconcilable elements of the American nature into a transcendental upper sphere.

European critics have never been able to understand why a "young nation," living a vigorous, primitive life, should not have expressed itself artistically in a cognate form; and because Whitman did so they accepted him as the representative poet of America. So he was; but it is only now, long after the pioneer epoch has passed and the "free note" has begun to make itself heard, that he has come to seem a typical figure to his own countrypeople. In his own time Whitman was regarded with distrust and even hatred because, by releasing, or tending to release, the creative faculties of the American mind, by exacting a poetical coöperation from his readers, he broke the pioneer law of self-preservation. By awakening people to their environment, by turning democracy from a fact into a spiritual principle, his influence ran directly counter to the necessities of the age, and his fellow-writers justly shunned him for hitting in this way below the belt. In fact, had Whitman continued to develop along the path he originally marked out for himself he might have seriously interfered with the logical process of the country's material evolution. But there was in Whitman himself a large share of the naïve pioneer nature, which made it impossible for him to take experience very seriously or to develop beyond a certain point. As he grew older, the sensuality of his nature led him astray in a vast satisfaction with material facts, before which he purred like a cat by the warm fire. This accounts for the reconciliation which occurred in later years between Whitman and his literary contemporaries. They saw that he had become harmless; they accepted him as a man of talent; and making the most of his more conventional verse, they

The Critics and Young America

at last crowned him provisionally as the "good gray poet."

For the orthodox writers of the old school had a serious duty to perform in speeding the pioneers on their way; and they performed it with an efficiency that won them the gratitude of all their contemporaries. Longfellow with his lullabies, crooning to sleep the insatiable creative appetites of the soul, Lowell, with his "weak-wing'd song" exalting "the deed" —how invaluable their literature was to the "tired pioneer," forerunner of the "tired business man" of the present day and only a loftier type because, like the tired soldier of the trenches, it was in response to the necessities of the race that he had dammed at their source the rejuvenating springs of the spirit! Yes, it was a great service those old writers rendered to the progress of this country's primitive development, for by unconsciously taking in charge, as it were, all the difficult elements of human nature and putting them under an anesthesia, they provided a free channel for the *élan* of their age.

But in so doing they shelved our spiritual life, conventionalizing it in a sphere above the

Van Wyck Brooks

sphere of action. In happier countries literature is the vehicle of ideals and attitudes that
have sprung from experience, ideals and attitudes that release the creative impulses of the
individual and stimulate a reaction in the
individual against his environment. This our
literature has failed to do; it has necessarily
remained an exercise rather than an expression.
Itself denied the principle of life or the power
of giving life, it has made up for its failure
to motivate the American scene and impreg-
nate it with meaning by concentrating all its
forces in the exterior field of esthetic form.
Gilding and idealizing everything it has
touched and frequently attaining a high level
of imaginative style, it has thrown veils over
the barrenness and emptiness of our life, putting us in extremely good conceit with ourselves while actually doing nothing either to
liberate our minds or to enlighten us as to the
real nature of our civilization. Hence we have
the meticulous technique of our contemporary
"high-class" magazines, a technique which, as
we know, can be acquired as a trick, and which,
artistic as it appears, is really the mark of a
complete spiritual conventionality and deceives

no sensible person into supposing that our general cleverness is the index of a really civilized society.

II

This total absence of any organic native culture has determined our response to the culture of the outer world. There are no vital relationships that are not reciprocal and only in the measure that we undergo a cognate experience ourselves can we share in the experience of others. To the Catholic, Dante, to the aristocrat, Nietzsche, to the democrat, Whitman, inevitably means more than any of them can mean to the scholar who merely receives them all through his intellect without the palpitant response of conviction and a sympathetic experience. Not that this "experience" has to be identical in the literal sense; no, the very essence of being cultivated is to have developed a capacity for sharing points of view other than our own. But there is all the difference between being actively and passively cultivated that there is between living actively or passively emotional lives. Only the creative mind can really apprehend the expressions of the creative mind. And it is because our field of action has been preëmpted by our acquisitive instincts, because in short we have no national fabric of spiritual experience, that we are so unable to-day to think and feel in international terms. Having ever considered it our prerogative to pluck the fruits of the spirit without undergoing the travail of generating them, having ever given to the tragi-comedy of the creative life a notional rather than a real assent, to quote Newman's famous phrase, we have been able to feed ourselves with the sugar-coating of all the bitter pills of the rest of mankind, accepting the achievements of their creative life as effects which presuppose in us no causal relationships. That is why we are so terribly at ease in the Zion of world culture.

All this explains the ascendancy among our fathers of the Arnoldian doctrine about "knowing the best that has been thought and said in the world." For, wrapped up as they were in their material tasks, it enabled them to share vicariously in the heritage of civilization, endowing them, as it were, with all the pearls of the oyster while neatly evading in their behalf the sad responsibility of the oyster itself. It upholstered their lives with everything that is best in history, with all mankind's most sumptuous effects quite sanitarily purged of their ugly and awkward organic relationships. It set side by side in the Elysian calm of their bookshelves all the warring works of the mighty ones of the past. It made the creative life synonymous in their minds with finished things, things that repeat their message over and over and "stay put." In short, it conventionalized for them the spiritual experience of humanity, pigeonholing it, as it were, and leaving them fancy-free to live "for practical purposes."

I remember that when as children we first read Carlyle and Ruskin we were extremely puzzled by their notes of exasperated indignation. "What are they so angry about?" we wondered, and we decided that England must be a very wicked country. Presently, however, even this idea passed out of our heads, and we came to the conclusion that anger and indignation must be simply normal properties of the literary mind (as they are, in a measure) and that we ought to be grateful for this because they produce so many engaging grotesqueries of style. Our own life was so obviously ship-shape and water-tight—was it possible that people in other countries could have allowed their life to become less so? Unable as we were to decide this point, we were quite willing to give the prophets the benefit of the doubt, as regards their own people. But it was inconceivable that for us they meant any more by their emotional somersaults than the prophets of the Bible meant, whose admirably intoned objurgations we drank in with perfect composure on Sundays.

How natural, then, that the greatest, the most "difficult" European writers should have had, as Carlyle and Browning and Meredith had, their first vogue in America! How natural that we should have flocked about Ibsen, patronized Nietzsche, found something entertaining in every kind of revolutionist, and welcomed the strangest philosophies (the true quite as readily as the false)! For having ourselves undergone no kindred creative experience for them to corroborate and extend, we have ever been able to escape their slings and arrows with a whole skin. They have said nothing real to us because there has been nothing in our own field of reality to make their messages real.

Consequently, those very European writers who might, under normal circumstances, have done the most to shake us out of our complacency have only served the more to confirm us in it. Our immediate sphere of action being sealed against them, their influence has been deflected into "mere literature," where it has not been actually inverted. For in so far as our spiritual appetites have been awake, it has only gone to convince us, not that we are unenlightened ourselves, but that other people are wicked. This explains the double paradox that while our reformers never consider it necessary to take themselves in hand before they set out to improve the world, our orthodox literary men, no matter what models they place before themselves, cannot rise above the tribal view of their art as either an amusement or a soporific.

Van Wyck Brooks

How then can our literature be anything but impotent? It is inevitably so, since it springs from a national mind that has been sealed against that experience from which literature derives all its values.

How true this is can be seen from almost any of its enunciations of principle, especially on the popular, that is to say the frankest, level. I open, for instance, one of our so-called better-class magazines and fall upon a character-sketch of William Gillette: "What a word! *Forget!* What a feat! What a faculty! Lucky the man who can himself forget. How gifted the one who can make others forget. It is the triumph of the art of William Gillette that in the magic of his spell an audience forgets." Opening another magazine, I turn to a reported interview in which a well-known popular poet expatiates on his craft. "Modern life," he tells us, "is full of problems, complex and difficult, and the man who concentrates his mind on his problems all day doesn't want to concentrate it on tediously obscure poetry at night. The newspaper poets are forever preaching the sanest optimism, designed for the people who really need the influence of optimism—the breadwinners, the weary, the heavy-laden. That's the kind of poetry the people want, and the fact that they want it shows that their hearts and heads are all right."

Here are two typical pronouncements of the American mind, one on the art of acting, one on the art of poetry, and they unite in expressing a perfectly coherent doctrine. This doctrine is that the function of art is to turn aside the problems of life from the current of emotional experience and create in its audience a condition of cheerfulness that is not organically derived from experience but added from the outside. It assumes that experience is not the stuff of life but something essentially meaningless; and not merely meaningless but an obstruction which retards and complicates our real business of getting on in the world and getting up in the world, and which must therefore be ignored and forgotten and evaded and beaten down by every means in our power.

What is true on the popular level is not less true on the level of serious literature, in spite

Van Wyck Brooks

of everything our most conscientious artists have been able to do. Thirty years ago an acute English critic remarked, apropos of a novel by Mr. Howells, that our novelists seemed to regard the Civil War as an occurrence that separated lovers, not as something that ought normally to have colored men's whole thoughts on life. And it is true that if we did not know how much our literature has to be discounted, we could hardly escape the impression, for all the documents which have come down to us, that our grandfathers really did pass through the war without undergoing the purgation of soul that is often said to justify the workings of tragic mischance in human affairs. Mr. Howells has himself given us the *comédie humaine* of our post-bellum society, Mr. Howells whose whole aim was to measure the human scope of that society and who certainly far less than any other novelist of his time falsified his vision of reality in the interests of popular entertainment. Well, we know the sort of society Mr. Howells pictured and how he pictured it. He has himself explicitly stated, in connection with certain Russian novels, that Americans in general do not

132

undergo the varieties of experience that Russian fiction records, that "the more smiling aspects of life" are "the more American," and that in being true to our "well-to-do actualities" the American novelist does all that can be expected of him. Could one ask for a more essential declaration of artistic bankruptcy than that?

For what does it amount to, this declaration? It identifies the reality of the artist's vision with what is accepted as reality in the world about him. But every one knows that the sketchiest, the most immature, the most trivial society is just as susceptible as any other of the most profound artistic reconstruction; all that is required is an artist capable of penetrating beneath it. The great artist floats the visible world on the sea of his imagination and measures it not according to its own scale of values but according to the values that he has himself derived from his descent into the abysses of life. What, then, is amiss with our writers? They are victims of the universal taboo which the ideal of material success, of the acquisitive life, has placed upon experience. It matters not at all that they have no

part or lot in this ideal, that they are men **of**
the finest artistic conscience. In the first place,
from their earliest childhood they are taught
to repress everything that conflicts with the
material welfare of their environment; in the
second place, their environment is itself so
denatured, so stripped of everything that might
nourish the imagination, that they do not so
much mature at all as externalize themselves
in a world of externalities. Unable to achieve
a sufficiently active consciousness of themselves
to return upon their environment and over-
throw it and dissolve it and re-create it in the
terms of a personal vision, they gradually come
to accept it on its own terms. If Boston is their
theme, they become Bostonian; if it is the
Yukon, they become "abysmal brutes"; if it
is nature, nature becomes the hero of their
work; and if it is machinery, the machines
themselves become vocal and express their natural contempt for a humanity that is incapable,
either morally or artistically, of putting them
in their place and keeping them there.

We know how this occurred with Mr. Howells. "It seemed to me then, and for a good
while afterward," he writes in *Literary Friends*

and Acquaintance, apropos of his first reception by the Boston Olympians of the 'sixties, "that a person who had seen the men and had the things said before him that I had in Boston, could not keep himself too carefully in cotton; and this was what I did all the following winter, though of course it was a secret between me and me." Never, assuredly, in any other society, has literary hero-worship taken quite the complexion of that; for the statement is accurately true. Such was the prestige of Boston and the pundits of Boston that Mr. Howells, having cast his anchor in its lee, never felt the necessity of exploring, on his own account, beyond the spacious, quiet harbor of life that presented itself to the cultivated New England eye. The result can be seen in such novels as *A Modern Instance*, the tragedy of which is viewed not from the angle of an experience that is wider and deeper, as the experience of a great novelist always is, than that of any character the novelist's imagination is able to conceive, but from the angle of Ben Halleck, the epitome of Boston's best public opinion. Boston passes judgment, and Mr. Howells concurs; and you close the book

135

feeling that you have seen life not through the eye of a free personality but of a highly conventional community at a given epoch.

It is exactly the same, to ignore a thousand incidental distinctions, in the work of Jack London. Between the superman of European fiction and Jack London's superman there is all the difference that separates an ideal achieved in the mind of the writer and a fact accepted from the world outside him; all the difference, in short, that separates the truth of art from the appearance of life. If these, therefore, among the freshest and most original talents our fiction has known since Hawthorne's day, have been absorbed in an atmosphere which no one has ever been able to condense, is it remarkable that the rank and file have slipped and fallen, that they have never learned to stand upright and possess themselves? Is it remarkable that they sell themselves out at the first bid, that they dress out their souls in the ready-made clothes the world offers them?

Such, in fact, is the deficiency of personal impulse, of the creative will, in America, so overwhelming is the demand laid upon Americans to serve ulterior and impersonal ends, that it is as if the springs of spiritual action had altogether evaporated. Launched in a society where individuals and their faculties appear only to pass away, almost wholly apart from and without acting upon one another, our writers find themselves enveloped in an impalpable atmosphere that acts as a perpetual dissolvent to the whole field of reality both within and without themselves, an atmosphere that invades every sphere of life and takes its discount from everything that they can do, an atmosphere that prevents the formation of oases of reality in the universal chaos. Is it remarkable that they take refuge in the abstract, the non-human, the impersonal, in the "bigness" of the phenomenal world, in the surface values of "local color," and in the "social conscience," which enables them to do so much good by writing badly that they often come to think of artistic truth itself as an enemy of progress?

IV

Thus, because it possesses none of those values which endow life with a significance in

and of itself, values which art and literature
alone can give, the American mind has been
gradually subdued to what it has worked in.
It has had no barriers to throw up against the
overwhelming material forces that have be-
leaguered it. Consequently, it has gone out of
itself as it were and assumed the values of
its environment.

Of this the most obvious example is the
peculiar optimism, the so-called systematic optimism, that can be fairly taken as what psychologists call the "total reaction upon life"
of the typical American mind of the last
twenty years. Mr. Horace Fletcher has defined this optimism in terms that leave no
doubt of its being at once an effect and a cause
of our spiritual impotence:

"Optimism can be prescribed and applied as
a medicine. Is there anything new and practical in this or is it but a continuation of the
endless discussion of the philosophy of life,
morals, medicine, etc.? Is it something that a
busy person may put into practice, take with
him to his business, without interfering with
his business, and profit by; and, finally, what
does it cost? Does adoption of it involve dis-

charging one's doctor-friend, displeasing one's
pastor, alienating one's social companions, or
shocking the sacred traditions that were dear
to father and mother? It is ameliorative, pre-
ventive, and harmonizing; and also it is easy,
agreeable, ever available, and altogether profitable. By these hall-marks of Truth we know
that it is true."

Grotesque as this may seem, you will search
in vain for a more accurate presentation of the
workaday point of view of our tumbling American world. This is the way Americans think,
and what they think, whether they profess the
religion of mind cure, uplift, sunshine, popular
pragmatism, the gospel of advertising, or plain
business; and they mean exactly what the
beauty experts mean when they say, "Avoid
strong emotions if you wish to retain a youth-
ful complexion." Systematic optimism, in
other words, effects a complete revaluation of
values and enthrones truth upon a conception
of animal success the prerequisite of which is
a thorough-going denial and evasion of emotional experience. It is the chronic result of
contact with a prodigal nature too easily borne
under by a too great excess of will, of oppor-

tunities so abundant and so alluring that we
have been led to suppress the creative spirit in
ourselves, traditionally unaware as we are of
the mature potentialities and justifications of
human nature, and establish our scale of values
in the incomparably rich material territory that
surrounds us. If to-day, therefore, we find no
principle of integrity at work in any department of our life, if religion competes with advertising, art competes with trade, and trade
gives itself out as philanthropy, if we present
to the world at large the spectacle of a vast undifferentiated herd of good-humored animals,
it is because we have passively surrendered our
human values at the demand of circumstance.

v

When I speak of the culture of industrialism I do not mean to imply that it has been
peculiar to us. Everywhere the industrial
process has devitalized men and produced a
poor quality of human nature. By virtue of
this process the culture of the whole Western
world fell too largely, during the nineteenth
century, into the hands of the prig and the

esthete, those two sick blossoms of the same
sapless stalk, whose roots have been for so long
unwatered by the convictions of the race. But
in Europe the great traditional culture, the
culture that has ever held up the flame of the
human spirit, has never been quite gutted out.
The industrialism that bowled us over, because
for generations our powers of resistance had
been undermined by Puritanism, was no sooner
well under way in Europe than human nature
began to get its back up, so to speak; and a
long line of great rebels reacted violently
against its desiccating influences. Philologists
like Nietzsche and Renan, digging among the
roots of Greek and Semitic thought, artists like
Morris and Rodin, rediscovering the beautiful
and happy art of the Middle Ages, economists
like Marx and Mill, revolting against the facts
of their environment, kept alive the tradition
of a great society and great ways of living and
thus were able to assimilate for human uses
the positive by-products of industrialism itself,
science and democracy. They made it impossible for men to forget the degradation of society and the poverty of their lives and built
a bridge between the greatness of the few in
141

the past and the greatness of the many, perhaps, in the future. Thus the democracies of
Europe are richer than ours in self-knowledge,
possessing ideals grounded in their own field
of reality and so providing them with a con-
stant stimulus to rise above their dead selves,
never doubting that experience itself is worth
having lived for, even if it leads to nothing
else. And thus, however slowly they advance,
they advance on firm ground.

For us, individually and socially, as I have
tried to show, nothing of this kind has been
possible. It seems to me wonderfully symbolic
of our society that the only son of Lincoln
should have become the president of the Pull-
man Company, that the son of the man who
liberated the slaves politically should have
been the first, as *The Nation* pointed out not
long ago, to exploit them industrially. Our
disbelief in experience, our habitual repression
of the creative instinct, our consequent over-
stimulation of the acquisitive instinct, has
made it impossible for us to take advantage
of the treasures our own life has yielded. Democracy and science, for example, have *happened to us* abundantly, more abundantly per-

haps than to others because they have had less
inertia to overcome; but like children presented with shining gold pieces we have not
known how to use them. Either we have been
unable to distinguish them from copper pen-
nies, or else we have spent them in foolish
ways that have made us ill. Our personal life
has in no way contributed to the enriching of
our environment; our environment, in turn,
has given us personally no sense of the significance of life.

We of the younger generation, therefore,
find ourselves in a grave predicament. For
having, unlike Europeans of any class, no fund
of spiritual experience in our blood as it were,
to balance the various parts of our natures,
we are all but incapable of coördinating ourselves in a free world. We are no longer able
to make the sort of "go" of life our fathers
made: the whole spirit of our age is against
the dualism which they accepted as a matter
of course. The acquisitive life has lost the
sanction of necessity which the age of pioneering gave it. A new age has begun, an age
of intensive cultivation, and it is the creative
life that the nation calls for now. But for

that how ill-equipped we are! Our literature has prepared no pathways for us, our leaders are themselves lost. We are like explorers who, in the morning of their lives, have deserted the hearthstone of the human tradition and have set out for a distant treasure that has turned to dust in their hands; but having on their way neglected to mark their track they no longer know in which direction their home lies, nor how to reach it, and so they wander in the wilderness, consumed with a double consciousness of waste and impotence.

I think this fairly describes the frame of mind of a vast number of Americans of the younger generation. They find themselves born into a race that has drained away all its spiritual resources in the struggle to survive and that continues to struggle in the midst of plenty because life itself no longer possesses any other meaning. The gradual commercialization of all the professions, meanwhile, has all but entirely destroyed the possibility of personal growth along the lines that our society provides and, having provided, sanctions. Brought up as they have been to associate activity almost solely with material ends and unable in this overwhelmingly prosperous age to feel any powerful incentive to seek these ends, acutely conscious of their spiritual unemployment and impoverished in will and impulse, the more sensitive minds of the younger generation drift almost inevitably into a state of internal anarchism that finds outlet, where it finds outlet at all, in a hundred unproductive forms.

Our society, in fact, which does everything by wholesale, is rapidly breeding a race of Hamlets the like of which has hardly been seen before, except perhaps in nineteenth-century Russia. Nothing is more remarkable than the similarity in this respect between the two immense inchoate populations that flank Europe on east and west. To be sure, the Oblomovs and Bazarovs and Levins and Dmitri Rudins of Russian fiction are in many ways, like Hamlet himself, universal characters. But for one Hamlet in an organized society which, according to the measure of its organization, provides an outlet for every talent, there are twenty in a society which, as we say, has no use for its highly developed types. And that is the situation both in Russia and the United States: the social fabric is too simple to be able to cope with the complicated strain that has been suddenly put upon it by a radical change in the conditions of life. Yet in each case the complexities have developed along just the lines most necessary for the rounded well-being of society. The Hamlets of Russian fiction, generally speaking, are social idealists, wrapped up in dreams of agricultural and educational reform; they long to revolutionize their country estates and ameliorate the lot of their peasantry, and they lose their will and their vision because there is no social machinery they can avail themselves of: thrown as they are upon their own unaided resources, their task overwhelms them at the outset with a sense of futility. Turn the tables about and you have the situation of the corresponding class in America. They find the machinery of education and social welfare in a state as highly developed as the life of the spirit is in Russia; it is the spiritual technique that is wanting, a living culture, a complicated scheme of ideal objectives, upheld by society at large, enabling them to submerge their liberties in their loyalties and to unite in the task of building up a civilization.

In short, owing to the miraculous rapidity and efficiency with which we have been able to effect the material conquest of the continent, a prodigious amount of energy has been thrown out of employment which our society is unable to receive and set to work. All the innate spirituality of the American nature, dammed up, stagnant from disuse, has begun to pour itself out in a vast flood of undisciplined emotionalism that goes—how often!—to waste. It goes to waste largely because the scope of our "useful" objectives is so restricted, and because, inheriting as we do an ingrained individualism, an ingrained belief in quick returns, we are all but unable to retain these treacherous elements, of which we have had so little practical experience in the past, until they have reached a sufficient maturity to take shape in lasting forms.

But this new individualism, which finds its gospel in self-expression, is totally different from the individualism of the past. The old spiritual individualism was blood-brother to

Van Wyck Brooks

the old materialistic individualism: it throve in
the same soil and produced a cognate type of
mind. It was hard, stiff-necked, combative,
opinionative, sectarian, self-willed; it gave
birth to the crank, the shrill, high-strung pro-
pounder of strange religions, the self-impor-
tant monopolist of truth. In short, it was
essentially competitive. The new individualism, on the other hand, is individualistic only
by default; its individualistic character, so to
say, is only an inherited bad habit, a bad habit
that is perpetuated by the want of objectives
in the truly vacuous world with which it finds
itself confronted. It has, I think, no desire to
vaunt itself; it tends, instead of this, to lavish
itself; it is not combative, it is coöperative,
not opinionative but groping, not sectarian but
filled with an intense, confused eagerness to
identify itself with the life of the whole people. If it remains confused, if it is unable to
discipline itself, if it is often lazy and wilful,
if its smoke is only at intervals illuminated by
flame—well, was it not just so with the Oblomovs of Russia? I can't conceive that any
one *wants* to be confused and lazy, especially
if he has no material motives to console him

in other ways. People who do not "burn with a hard, gem-like flame" are simply people who are not being employed by civilization.

Undoubtedly the gospel of self-expression, makeshift as it is, has revealed a promise in America that we have always taken for granted but hardly reckoned with. Isolated, secretive, bottled up as we have been in the past, how could we ever have guessed what aims and hopes we have in common had they not been brought to light, even in the crudest and most inadequate ways? That they have at last been brought to light I think few will deny; but will they get any further? Only, it seems to me, if we are able to build up, to adapt a phrase from the slang of politics, a programme for the conservation of our spiritual resources.

"Humanity," wrote Mazzini in 1858, "is a great army marching to the conquest of unknown lands, against enemies both strong and cunning. The peoples are its corps, each with its special operation to carry out, and the common victory depends on the exactness with which they execute the different operations." That nationalities are the workshops of humanity, that each nationality has a special

149

Van Wyck Brooks

duty to perform, a special genius to exert, a special gift to contribute to the general stock of civilization, and that each, in consequence, growing by the trust that other nationalities place in it, must be a living, homogeneous entity, with its own faith and consciousness of self—could any idea more perfectly than this express the dream, the necessity, of Young America? To live creatively, to live completely, to live in behalf of some great corporate purpose,—that is its desire. A national faith we had once, a national dream, the dream of the "great American experiment." But had it not been sadly compromised would the younger generation find itself adrift as it is today? Too many elements of that old faith of ours were at war with all that was good in it, and it admitted so few of the factors of life; it was betrayed by what was false within; it was unable to embrace the freer impulses of a new time. That is why it contributes so little to the new faith without which America cannot live.

To discover that faith, to formulate that new technique, to build up, as I have said, that programme for the conservation of our spiritual resources, is the task of American criticism. Let it first observe the "object" and the conditions of the object. It should then be able to make the "situation."

Genius and Taste[1]

By IRVING BABBITT

I

IN *Roderick Random* (1748), the poet Melo-
poyn, confined in the Marshalsea for debt,
stalks forth "wrapped in a dirty rug tied about
his loins with two pieces of list of different
colors," and, making a profound bow to the
assembled prisoners, pronounces before them
"with great significance of voice and gesture
a very elegant and ingenious discourse upon
the difference between genius and taste." Mr.
Spingarn's views on genius and taste, in his
Creative Criticism, like so many other views
that are being put forth as ultra-modern, take
us back to this period in the eighteenth century. A new movement began to gain head
about that time, a movement in the midst of
which we are still living, and the opposition
between this movement and traditional con-

[1] Reprinted from *The Nation* of February 7, 1918.

ceptions appears nowhere more clearly, perhaps, than in its reinterpretation of such words as genius and taste. In one of his most conservative moods Voltaire defined genius as only "judicious imitation"; which meant in practice the imitation of the approved models according to certain rules and conventions. But to imitate thus is to be merely orthodox, and Voltaire maintains that after all mere orthodoxy, though necessary, does not suffice. In any one who hopes to achieve literary salvation good works must be supplemented by grace, and grace is accorded to but few. If Voltaire is to the last degree astringent and restrictive in his attitude towards literary genius, he is hardly less so in his attitude towards taste. The critic, too, he holds, must have a special tact and intuition that cannot be acquired. Voltaire estimates that in the whole world there are only a few thousand men of taste—mainly settled about Paris. In short, genius and taste as Voltaire views them are very vivid and vital things, but operate within the limits imposed by the neo-classic doctrine of imitation, a doctrine that suffered from the start from a taint of formalism.

Irving Babbitt

Those who sought to purge literature of this taint began towards the middle of the eighteenth century to oppose to the neo-classical harping on judgment and imitation a plea for imagination and originality. The enthusiast and original genius who emerged at this time and arrayed himself against the wit and man of the world had from the outset a strong leaning towards primitivism. For example, Edward Young's *Conjectures on Original Composition* (1759) will be found in its attacks on imitation, and its exaltation of spontaneity and free expression, to anticipate surprisingly the gospel of recent primitivists like Mr. Spingarn and his master, Benedetto Croce. According to the older school, art aims not at the expression of the individual, but at the universal—the "grandeur of generality." On the contrary, says Young, genius resides in one's ultimate idiosyncrasy, that ineffable something that makes every man different from his fellows. If one wishes to be a creator and not a mechanical imitator, one should simply be one's temperamental self, and above all submit to no constraint upon one's imagination. "In the fairyland of fancy genius may wander wild; there it

154

Genius and Taste

has a creative power and may reign arbitrarily over its own empire of chimeras." (The empire of chimeras was later to become the tower of ivory.) If one is not to be contaminated by imitation, it is an advantage, Young insinuates, to be ignorant and brainless. "Many a genius probably there has been which could neither write nor read." This advantage, the primitivist soon came to argue, was enjoyed especially in the early stages of society before originality had been crushed beneath a superincumbent weight of artificial culture, and before critics had begun their pernicious activities. This primitivistic view of genius received a great stimulus from the publication of the Ossianic poems. "Genius," says Diderot, summing up a whole movement, "calls for something enormous, primitive and barbaric."

If genius, according to the primitivist, is something purely expressive, a spontaneous temperamental overflow, taste, as he views it, is likewise at the opposite pole from the taste of the neo-classicist. Voltaire failed to do justice to certain writers—Shakespeare, for example—who were outside the strict neo-classical convention. According to the new doctrine, the

155

critic should cease to be thus exclusive and become comprehensive and sympathetic. This is an important half-truth, though perhaps no half-truth since the beginning of the world has ever been so overworked. For it is not enough, as Mr. Spingarn would have us believe, that the critic should ask what the creator aimed to do and whether he has fulfilled his aim; he must also ask whether the aim is intrinsically worth while. He must, in other words, rate creation with reference to some standard set both above his own temperament and that of the creator. According to the primitivist, on the contrary, the genius has simply to let himself go both imaginatively and emotionally, and the whole business of the critic is to receive so keen an impression from the resulting expression that when passed through his temperament it issues forth as a fresh expression. By thus participating in the creative thrill of genius, the critic becomes creative in turn, and in so far genius and taste are one.

Now taste has been defined as a man's literary conscience. The transformation of the literary conscience that took place in the

eighteenth century is only one aspect of the
transformation that took place during that
period in the conscience in general. Instead of
being looked upon, as it always had been traditionally, as an inner check upon impulse and
emotion, the conscience came to be regarded as
itself an expansive emotion. Once discredit the
veto power in human nature, once identify the
spirit that says no with the devil, and the rest
—for example, the tendency of genius and taste
to run together in a common expansiveness, a
common eagerness for expression—follows
quickly. "The identity of genius and taste,"
says Mr. Spingarn, "is the final achievement
of modern thought on the subject of art;
and it means that fundamentally the creative
and critical instincts are one and the same."
In that case the credit of this discovery belongs
to critics who antedate by at least a century
Signor Croce. For example, A. W. Schlegel
protests in his Berlin lectures (1803) against
a "fault-finding criticism that looked upon
what is truly positive in poetry—genius—as
the evil principle, and wished to subordinate
it to the negative principle—so-called good

taste; an unreal and purely fanciful contrast.
These two things (*i.e.*, genius and taste) are
indivisibly one."

II

If the creator has merely to get his own
genius, *i.e.*, his own uniqueness, expressed, it
is hard to see why the critic should be more
disinterested, why he should not be less concerned with the faithfulness of the impression
he receives from the work of the creator than
with the temperamental modifications he gives
this impression, with his remolding of it into
a fresh creation so that it may become expressive of *his* genius. These ultimate implications
of the expressionistic-impressionistic view have
been worked out by no one more consistently,
perhaps, than by Oscar Wilde in his dialogue
The Critic as Artist. "Criticism," Wilde con-
cludes, "is the only civilized form of autobiog-
raphy." Except that he falls somewhat short
of this last affirmation, Mr. Spingarn runs very
closely parallel to Wilde, to whom indeed he
makes due acknowledgment. What underlies
this whole movement from the original genius

of the eighteenth century down to Wilde and
Mr. Spingarn is the craving for an indeter-
minate vagabondage of imagination and emotion; and far more significant than the emotional emancipation is the emancipation of the
imagination from any allegiance to standards,
from any central control. The neo-classicists
had forgotten in their devotion to what they
conceived to be truth and nature, by which they
meant normal human nature, the supreme rôle
of the imagination, or, if one prefers, of illusion
in both art and life. They hoped, as we have
seen, to achieve their grandeur of generality by
a merely judicious imitation. Yet Voltaire
himself had declared that "illusion is the queen
of the human heart." The original genius opposed to the unimaginative neo-classic notion of
normality an imagination that is subject to no
norm whatsoever, that is, in Young's phrase,
free to wander wild in its own empire of
chimeras. Wilde has the supreme effrontery to
put this cult of pure illusion under the patron-
age of Aristotle. But this should at least serve
to remind us that Aristotle, unlike the neo-
classicists, recognizes the all-important rôle of
illusion. The poet, he says, gives us a truth

superior to that of the historian—superior because it is more representative. But in order
to give us this representative truth, he goes on
to say, the poet must be a master of illusion.
In Goethe's phrase, the best art gives us "the
illusion of a higher reality"; and this has the
advantage of being strictly experimental, of
being only a statement of what one actually
experiences on reading a great poem or seeing
a great picture. Imitation, in the theory of an
Aristotle and the practice of a Sophocles or a
Phidias, is not merely judicious, but creative,
and creative because it is imaginative. For the
Greek, genius consists not in getting one's
uniqueness uttered, but in the imaginative perception of the universal. Homer, says Aristotle, is the greatest of poets because he never
entertains us with his own person, but is the
most constantly an imitator. Homer still remains the greatest of poets for this very reason.
He paints with his eye on the object, and that
object is human nature.

The opposite pole is reached when Lamar-
tine tells us that he wrote solely for "the relief
of his heart." The fact that the poet who
overflows in this way is widely acclaimed is

no sure proof that he has attained the universal.
Many men may become abnormal at the same
time and in the same way. A whole generation
saw itself reflected in *René*. *René* is already
more remote from us than Homer; and that is
because the quality of the imagination dis-
played is, from the point of view of normal
human experience, highly eccentric. It has
been said, on the other hand, that Shakespeare
dwells at the very centre of human nature.
This is only another way of saying that Shakespeare is one of the most imaginative of men.
His imagination, however, is not irresponsible
like that of the original genius, but is disciplined to reality. At his best he is ethical in
the Greek sense. To be ethical in the Greek
sense is not to preach or to agitate problems,
but to see life with imaginative wholeness. It
is only too plain that the original genius, in
his break with the neo-classic formalist, did
not rise to ethical standards—to do this he
would have needed to work out a sound view
of the imagination and of imaginative imitation—but merely fell from legalism into anarchy. One should add—and this again is a
fact that every one can verify for himself—

Irving Babbitt

that the highest type of creator gets his general truth without any sacrifice of his peculiar personal note; he is at once unique and universal. But the original genius tends to identify—here is his underlying error—the normal with the commonplace. What he sees at the centre is academic routine, and he gets as far away from this centre as he can by inbreeding idiosyncrasy. And then somebody finds that the eccentric position thus assumed is still too central and proceeds to fly off from it; whereupon still another comes along and secedes from this seceder from a secessionist, and so on indefinitely. The extremists in painting have got so far beyond Cézanne, who was regarded not long ago as one of the wildest of innovators, that Cézanne is in a fair way, we read, to "achieve the unhappy fate of becoming a classic."

One should indeed not forget that in the house of art are many mansions. The imagination that is more or less free to wander wild in its own empire of chimeras has its place on the recreative side of life. The question of truth and reality is not in this sort of creation primary. But it is right here that the primi-

Genius and Taste

tivist is guilty of the gravest confusions. Mr.
Spingarn holds that the would-be creator
should submit to no test of truth and reality,
but should simply "let himself go" emotionally
and imaginatively; should get rid of "inner or
outer inhibitions," and the result, one is to believe, will not be something more or less re-crea-
tive; on the contrary, one will presently find
Mr. Spingarn crediting the creator of this type
with a "vision of reality" and "spiritual exaltation." Mr. Spingarn promises us that if we
follow his prescription, we shall not only have
genius—which will turn out to be identical
with taste—but that we shall also go mad.
One may agree with him that the man who
puts no check on his imagination, and is at the
same time convinced of his "spiritual exaltation," is in a fair way to go mad, but one may
disagree with him in deeming this madness a
divine madness. In its mildest forms this
whole theory of genius and taste encourages
conceit; in its more advanced forms megalomania. Once eliminate the high impersonal
standard, the ethical norm that sets bounds to
the eagerness of the creator to express himself,
and the eagerness of the creator to thrill to this

163

expression, and it is hard to see what measure of a man's merit is left save his intoxication with himself; and this measure would scarcely seem to be trustworthy. Virgil, we are told, wished to burn the Æneid. The undergraduate, on the other hand, often has a considerable conceit of his own genius in writing his daily theme. "Every ass that's romantic," says Wolseley in his preface to *Valentinian* (1685), "believes he's inspired."

After all, the doctrine of imitation merely means that one needs to look up to some standard set above one's ordinary self. Any one who looked up to the standards established by the two great traditions, the classical and the Christian, tended to acquire in some measure the supreme Christian virtue, humility, and the supreme classical virtue, decorum, or, if one prefers, a sense of proportion. To repudiate the traditional Christian and classical checks and at the same time fail to work out some new and more vital control upon impulse and temperament is to be guilty of high treason to civilization.

If, on the one hand, the "spiritual exaltation" of the primitivist makes against the two

164

virtues that sum up in a way all civilization, humility, and decorum, on the other hand it encourages the two root diseases of human nature, conceit and laziness. Mr. Spingarn's exhortation to get rid of both inner and outer inhibitions and let ourselves go amounts in effect to this: follow the line of least resistance —and be a genius. It is easy to be an unchained temperament, difficult to attain to a proportionate and disciplined view of life. By preaching sheer imaginative and emotional unrestraint in the name of expression, Mr. Spingarn is tending to discredit that very modern spirit [1] for which he professes to stand. If to be modern means anything, it means to be positive and experimental in one's attitude towards life. If such a phrase as a "vision of reality" is to have any experimental content, if it is to be anything more than a mask for egotism, the reality of which one has a vision will serve to set bounds to the expansion of one's ordinary self; will be known practically, in short, as an inner inhibition. It

[1] For my definition of the modern spirit see *Nation*, August 2, 1917 (article on "Matthew Arnold"). For my use of the word laziness see *ibid.*, October 18, 1917 ("Interpreting India to the West").

should be clear to any one who considers the case of those who have viewed life with some degree of centrality and wholeness that they have won their restraining ethical insight with the aid of the imagination. If a sound type of individualism is to be achieved, and this is the specifically modern problem, it is scarcely possible to stress too strongly the rôle of the ethical or generalizing imagination. Such vision of reality as is vouchsafed to finite man must ever come to him through a veil of illusion. This inseparableness of reality and illusion may embarrass the metaphysician, but not the positivist who discriminates between the sham vision and the true, not on metaphysical grounds, but by their fruits.

Now the fruits of the primitivistic theory of genius and originality have had time to become manifest. If this theory was incubated in eighteenth-century England, it received its chief developments in eighteenth-century Germany, where it was applied by Herder, Fichte, and others, not merely to individuals, but to nations. When an individual becomes unduly exalted over his own "genius," there are various ways in which he may be relieved of his

Genius and Taste

excess of conceit. But when a whole nation gets into a similar state of exaltation and is consumed by the ardor for self-expression, when instead of submission to genuine ethical standards there is a collective inbreeding of temperament and idiosyncrasy, then the case is well-nigh hopeless. One may then properly raise the question that Bishop Butler is said to have debated with himself, whether a whole nation may not go mad. National conceit runs into national megalomania, and the intoxication of a whole people with itself finally comes to be felt by it as an ecstatic "idealism." A nation of this kind may count upon having its "creative" critics, who will hope to show their taste by simply sharing this intoxication and their genius by giving it fresh expression.

III

This whole conception of genius and taste has about it the flavor of a decadent estheticism. The term creative critic, in particular, seems destined to remain a noteworthy example of what Arnold calls the grand name without the grand thing; and this is a pity, for there is an

167

important sense in which the critic should be creative, especially in an age like the present, which has cut loose from its traditional moorings. Before determining what this sense is, let us consider for a moment the true relation between creator and critic, between genius and taste. Not to speak of other and minor differences, the creator differs above all from the critic, not merely in having genius in general, but a mysterious and incommunicable gift. Dr. Johnson goes too far when he defines genius as "only a mind of large general powers accidentally determined to some particular direction." The musical genius of a Mozart, for example, cannot be accounted for in any such fashion. Dr. Johnson was nevertheless right in condemning the whole primitivistic notion of genius and the lazy drifting with temperament that it encouraged. As a seventeenth-century Frenchman put it, it is not enough to have great gifts, one must also know how to manage them. Though a man's genius may not be in his power, the control of this genius to some human end largely is. To determine this end, he must look to standards, standards which, if he is not to be a mere traditionalist, he must create with

Genius and Taste

the aid of the ethical imagination. If he does not seek to humanize his gift, if he is content to be a mere unchained force of nature, he may have genius, almost any amount of it, and yet remain, as Tennyson said of Hugo, only a "weird Titan."

The critic, for his part, cannot afford any more than the creator simply to let himself go. If he is merely content to partake of the creative thrill of genius, he may have gusto, zest, relish, what you will, but he will not have taste. He will begin to have taste only when he refers the creative expression and his impression of it to some standard that is set above both. And if this standard is to be purified of every taint of formalism, it must not be merely traditional or rationalistic, but must rest on an immediate perception of what is normal and human, a perception that the critic, like the creator, can win in its fullness only with the aid of the ethical or generalizing imagination. The best type of critic may therefore be said to be creative in the sense that he creates standards. It is in their common allegiance to standards that critic and creator really come together. They ascend, and not, as in the primitivistic

169

theory, descend, to meet. With the elimination of the restrictive and selective principle—and the presence of standards is always felt as such a principle—what is left is the most dangerous of all forms of anarchy—anarchy of the imagination. This is what Goethe meant when he said that "nothing is so horrible as imagination without taste."

To acquire a true literary conscience, to mediate between the restrictive and selective principle and one's vivid personal impression, to have standards and then to apply them flexibly and intuitively, is not easy. It is to be feared that Voltaire is nearer the truth when he discourses on the small number of the elect in matters of taste than Mr. Spingarn when he utters his facile assurance, so agreeable to democratic ears, that "we are all geniuses; we are all possessed of taste." Mr. Spingarn's message would seem to be the very opposite of what we need in America at the present time. For though we no doubt have "ideals"—at least we seem very certain on this point—we lack standards; and the pathway to standards would scarcely seem to lie through the glorification of impulse and unrestraint. Because certain barriers imposed by neo-classic good taste were found to be arbitrary and artificial, the primitivist assumes that all barriers are arbitrary and artificial; and the consequences of this assumption, if worked out consistently, should give us pause. Civilization, at bottom, rests on the recognition of the fact that man shows his true liberty by resisting impulse, and not by yielding to it, that he grows in the perfection proper to his own nature not by throwing off but by taking on limitations. As a matter of fact, not much is left of the values of civilized life when Mr. Spingarn has finished enumerating the things that must be thrown overboard if the creator is to express himself adequately, and the "new" or "esthetic" critic is to partake of the creator's thrill and reëxpress it. Mr. Spingarn says that the opening night of the International Exhibition (1913) was one of the most "exciting adventures" that he had ever experienced. Many of the pictures that have been appearing in this and similar exhibitions of late years, far from being so excitingly novel, would suggest rather that our American partisans of pure expression are coming in at a late stage of a movement that from its rise in the

eighteenth century was unable to distinguish
between the original and the aboriginal. If
Mr. Theodore Dreiser, author of *The Genius*,
had set forth his views of originality in Germany about 1775 (*die Geniezeit*), they would
have been wrong, but they would at least have
had the semblance of novelty. As it is, it is
hard for a person even moderately versed in
literary history to read these views without
yawning. Nothing is more tiresome than stale
eccentricity. Is this country always to be the
dumping ground of Europe? Americans who
wish to display real virility and initiative will
scarcely be content to fall in at the end of the
procession, especially when the procession is
moving, as in this case, towards the edge of a
precipice. They will see that we must begin
by creating standards, if our other attempts at
creation are to have any meaning, and they
will not underestimate the difficulty of the task.
Primitivism leads to affirmations that are re-
pugnant to the most elementary common-sense
—for example, to Mr. Spingarn's affirmation
that the "art of a child is art quite as much as
that of Michelangelo." But it is not enough to

oppose to such aberrations mere common-sense or reason or judgment. The strength of the primitivist is that he recognizes in his own way the truth proclaimed by Napoleon—that imagination governs the world. Those who believe in the need of a humanistic reaction at present should be careful not to renew the neo-classical error. Thus Dryden attributes the immortality of the Æneid to its being "a well-weighed, judicious poem. Whereas poems which are produced by the vigor of imagination only have a gloss upon them at the first which time wears off, the works of judgment are like the diamond: the more they are polished the more luster they receive." But what is pre-eminent in Virgil, what gives the immortalizing touch to his work, is not the judgment he displays, but the quality of his imagination. It is no doubt inevitable, in speaking and writing, to divide man up into faculties and contrast judgment with imagination. At the same time one should recollect that this division of man into more or less water-tight compartments has about it nothing positive and experimental. What is positive and experimental, let me repeat, is that in creation of the first order, creation that has high seriousness in the Aristotelian sense, the imagination does not wander aimlessly, but is at work in the service of a supersensuous truth that it is not given to man to seize directly; and that the result is "the illusion of a higher reality." Creation of this order, one may report from actual observation, is something more than the intense expression of some expansive ego, whether individual or national; it has a restrained and humanized intensity—intensity on a background of calm. Our whole modern experiment, not only in art and literature, but in life, is threatened with breakdown, because of our failure to work out new standards with the aid of this type of imagination. And this breakdown of the modern experiment is due to its not having lived up to its own program. Those who have put aside the discipline of outer authority have professed to do so because of their thirst for immediacy, of their wish to face unflinchingly the facts of nature and of human nature. Yet the veto power in human nature is nothing abstract, nothing that one needs to take on hearsay, but a matter of immediate perception. It is this fact, the weightiest of all, that the corrupters of the literary conscience and of the conscience in general have failed to face in making of the imagination the irresponsible accomplice of the unchained emotions.

Criticism of Criticism of Criticism [1]

By H. L MENCKEN

EVERY now and then, a sense of the futility of their daily endeavors falling suddenly upon them, the critics of Christendom turn to a somewhat sour and depressing consideration of the nature and objects of their own craft. That is to say, they turn to criticizing criticism. What is it in plain words? What is its aim, exactly stated in legal terms? How far can it go? What good can it do? What is its normal effect upon the artist and the work of art?

Such a spell of self-searching has been in progress for several years past, and the critics of various countries have contributed theories of more or less lucidity and plausibility to the discussion. Their views of their own art, it appears, are quite as divergent as their views

[1] Originally published in the New York *Evening Mail*, July 1, 1918; reprinted with considerable revision in 1919 in *Prejudices, First Series*, and here reprinted by special arrangement with Alfred A. Knopf, Inc., authorized publishers.

of the arts they more commonly deal with. One group argues, partly by direct statement and partly by attacking all other groups, that the one defensible purpose of the critic is to encourage the virtuous and oppose the sinful— in brief, to police the fine arts and so hold them in tune with the moral order of the world. Another group, repudiating this constabulary function, argues hotly that the arts have nothing to do with morality whatsoever—that their concern is solely with pure beauty. A third group holds that the chief aspect of a work of art, particularly in the field of literature, is its aspect as psychological document—that if it doesn't help men to know themselves it is nothing. A fourth group reduces the thing to an exact science, and sets up standards that resemble algebraic formulæ—this is the group of metrists, of contrapuntists and of those who gabble of light-waves. And so, in order, follow groups five, six, seven, eight, nine, ten, each with its theory and its proofs.

Against the whole corps, moral and esthetic, psychological and algebraic, stands Major J. E. Spingarn, U.S.A. Major Spingarn lately served formal notice upon me that he had abandoned the life of the academic grove for that of the armed array, and so I give him his military title, but at the time he wrote his *Creative Criticism* he was a professor in Columbia University, and I still find myself thinking of him, not as a soldier extraordinarily literate, but as a professor in rebellion. For his notions, whatever one may say in opposition to them, are at least magnificently unprofessorial—they fly violently in the face of the principles that distinguish the largest and most influential group of campus critics. As witness: "To say that poetry is moral or immoral is as meaningless as to say that an equilateral triangle is moral and an isosceles triangle immoral." Or, worse: "It is only conceivable in a world in which dinner-table conversation runs after this fashion: 'This cauliflower would be good if it had only been prepared in accordance with international law.'" One imagines, on hearing such atheism flying about, the amazed indignation of Prof. Dr. William Lyon Phelps, with his discovery that Joseph Conrad preaches "the axiom of the moral law"; the "Hey, what's that!" of Prof. Dr. W. C. Brownell, the Amherst Aristotle, with his eloquent plea for stand-

Criticism of Criticism of Criticism

ards as iron-clad as the Westminster Confession; the loud, patriotic alarm of the gifted Prof. Dr. Stuart P. Sherman, of Iowa, with his maxim that Puritanism is the official philosophy of America, and that all who dispute it are enemy aliens and should be deported. Major Spingarn, in truth, here performs a treason most horrible upon the reverend order he once adorned, and having achieved it, he straightway performs another and then another. That is to say, he tackles all the antagonistic groups of orthodox critics seriatim, and knocks them about unanimously—first the aforesaid agents of the sweet and pious; then the advocates of unities, meters, all rigid formulæ; then the experts in imaginary psychology; then the historical comparers, pigeonholers and makers of categories; finally, the professors of pure esthetic. One and all, they take their places upon his operating table, and one and all they are stripped and anatomized.

But what is the anarchistic ex-professor's own theory?—for a professor must have a theory, as a dog must have fleas. In brief, what he offers is a doctrine borrowed from the Italian, Benedetto Croce, and by Croce filched from

179

H. L. Mencken

Goethe—a doctrine anything but new in the world, even in Goethe's time, but nevertheless long buried in forgetfulness—to wit, the doctrine that it is the critic's first and only duty, as Carlyle once put it, to find out "what the poet's aim really and truly was, how the task he had to do stood before his eye, and how far, with such materials as were afforded him, he has fulfilled it." For poet, read artist, or, if literature is in question, substitute the Germanic word *Dichter*—that is, the artist in words, the creator of beautiful letters, whether in verse or in prose. Ibsen always called himself a *Digter*, not a *Dramatiker* or *Skuespiller*. So, I dare say, did Shakespeare. . . . Well, what is this generalized poet trying to do? asks Major Spingarn, and how has he done it? That, and no more, is the critic's quest. The morality of the work does not concern him. It is not his business to determine whether it heeds Aristotle or flouts Aristotle. He passes no judgment on its rhyme scheme, its length and breadth, its iambics, its politics, its patriotism, its piety, its psychological exactness, its good taste. He may note these things, but he may not protest about them—he may not complain if the thing criticized fails to fit into a pigeonhole. Every sonnet, every drama, every novel is *sui generis;* it must stand on its own bottom; it must be judged by its own inherent intentions. "Poets," says Major Spingarn, "do not really write epics, pastorals, lyrics, however much they may be deceived by these false abstractions; they express *themselves, and this expression is their only form.* There are not, therefore, only three or ten or a hundred literary kinds; there are as many kinds as there are individual poets." Nor is there any valid appeal *ad hominem.* The character and background of the poet are beside the mark; the poem itself is the thing. Oscar Wilde, weak and swine-like, yet wrote beautiful prose. To reject that prose on the ground that Wilde had filthy habits is as absurd as to reject *What Is Man?* on the ground that its theology is beyond the intelligence of the editor of the New York *Times.*

This Spingarn-Croce-Carlyle-Goethe theory, of course, throws a heavy burden upon the critic. It presupposes that he is a civilized and tolerant man, hospitable to all intelligible ideas and capable of reading them as he runs. This is a demand that at once rules out nine-tenths

181

of the grown-up sophomores who carry on the business of criticism in America. Their trouble is simply that they lack the intellectual resilience necessary for taking in ideas, and particularly new ideas. The only way they can ingest one is by transforming it into the nearest related formula—usually a harsh and devastating operation. This fact accounts for their chronic inability to understand all that is most personal and original and hence most forceful and significant in the emerging literature of the country. They can get down what has been digested and redigested, and so brought into forms that they know, and carefully labeled by predecessors of their own sort—but they exhibit alarm immediately they come into the presence of the extraordinary. Here we have an explanation of Brownell's loud appeal for a tightening of standards—*i.e.*, a larger respect for precedents, patterns, rubber-stamps—and here we have an explanation of Phelps's inability to comprehend the colossal phenomenon of Dreiser, and of Boynton's childish nonsense about realism, and of Sherman's effort to apply the Espionage Act to the arts, and of More's querulous enmity to romanticism, and of all

Criticism of Criticism of Criticism

the fatuous pigeonholing that passes for criticism in the more solemn literary periodicals.

As practiced by all such learned and diligent but essentially ignorant and unimaginative men, criticism is little more than a branch of homiletics. They judge a work of art, not by its clarity and sincerity, not by the force and charm of its ideas, not by the technical virtuosity of the artist, not by his originality and artistic courage, but simply and solely by his orthodoxy. If he is what is called a "right thinker," if he devotes himself to advocating the transient platitudes in a sonorous manner, then he is worthy of respect. But if he lets fall the slightest hint that he is in doubt about any of them, or, worse still, that he is indifferent, then he is a scoundrel, and hence, by their theory, a bad artist. Such pious piffle is horribly familiar among us. I do not exaggerate its terms. You will find it running through the critical writings of practically all the dull fellows who combine criticism with tutoring; in the words of many of them it is stated in the plainest way and defended with much heat, theological and pedagogical. In its baldest form it shows itself in the doctrine that it is

scandalous for an artist—say a dramatist or a
novelist—to depict vice as attractive. The fact
that vice, more often than not, undoubtedly *is*
attractive—else why should it ever gobble any
of us?—is disposed of with a lofty gesture.
What of it? say these birchmen. The artist is
not a reporter, but a Great Teacher. It is not
his business to depict the world as it is, but as
it ought to be.

Against this notion American criticism makes
but feeble headway. We are, in fact, a nation
of evangelists; every third American devotes
himself to improving and lifting up his fellow-
citizens, usually by force; the messianic delusion is our national disease. Thus the moral
Privatdozenten have the crowd on their side,
and it is difficult to shake their authority; even
the vicious are still in favor of crying vice
down. "Here is a novel," says the artist.
"Why didn't you write a tract?" roars the
professor—and down the chute go novel and
novelist. "This girl is pretty," says the painter.
"But she has left off her undershirt," protests
the head-master—and off goes the poor dauber's
head. At its mildest, this balderdash takes the
form of the late Hamilton Wright Mabie's

Criticism of Criticism of Criticism

White List of Books; at its worst, it is com-
stockery, an idiotic and abominable thing.
Genuine criticism is as impossible to such in-
ordinately narrow and cocksure men as music
is to a man who is tone-deaf. The critic, to
interpret his artist, even to understand his artist,
must be able to get into the mind of his artist;
he must feel and comprehend the vast pressure
of the creative passion; as Major Spingarn says,
"Esthetic judgment and artistic creation are instinct with the same vital life." This is why
all the best criticism of the world has been
written by men who have had within them, not
only the reflective and analytical faculty of
critics, but also the gusto of artists—Goethe,
Carlyle, Lessing, Schlegel, Sainte-Beuve, and,
to drop a story or two, Hazlitt, Hermann Bahr,
Georg Brandes and James Huneker. Huneker,
tackling *Also sprach Zarathustra,* revealed its
content in illuminating flashes. But tackled
by Paul Elmer More, it became no more than
a dull student's exercise, ill-naturedly cor-
rected.

So much for the theory of Major J. E. Spingarn, U.S.A., late professor of comparative literature in Columbia University. Obviously, it

185

is a far sounder and more stimulating theory
than any of those cherished by the other professors. It demands that the critic be a man
of intelligence, of toleration, of wide information, of genuine hospitality to ideas, whereas
the others only demand that he have learning,
and accept anything as learning that has been
said before. But once he has stated his doctrine, the ingenious ex-professor, professor-like,
immediately begins to corrupt it by claiming
too much for it. Having laid and hatched, so
to speak, his somewhat stale but still highly
nourishing egg, he begins to argue fatuously
that the resultant flamingo is the whole muster-
ing of the critical *Aves*. But the fact is, of
course, that criticism, as humanly practiced,
must needs fall a good deal short of this intuitive recreation of beauty, and what is more, it
must go a good deal further. For one thing,
it must be interpretation in terms that are not
only exact but are also comprehensible to the
reader, else it will leave the original mystery
as dark as before—and once interpretation
comes in, paraphrase and transliteration come
in. What is recondite must be made plainer;
the transcendental, to some extent at least, must

186

Criticism of Criticism of Criticism

be done into common modes of thinking.
Well, what are morality, trochaics, hexameters,
movements, historical principles, psychological
maxims, the dramatic unities—what are all
these save common modes of thinking, short-
cuts, rubber stamps, words of one syllable?
Moreover, beauty as we know it in this world
is by no means the apparition *in vacuo* that
Mr. Spingarn seems to see. It has its social, its
political, even its moral implications. The
finale of Beethoven's C minor symphony is not
only colossal as music; it is also colossal as revolt; it says something against something. Yet
more, the springs of beauty are not within itself
alone, nor even in genius alone, but often in
things without. Brahms wrote his Deutsches
Requiem, not only because he was a great artist,
but also because he was a good German. And
in Nietzsche there are times when the divine
afflatus takes a back seat, and the *spirochaetae*
have the floor.

Major Spingarn himself seems to harbor
some sense of this limitation on his doctrine.
He gives warning that "the poet's intention
must be judged at the moment of the creative
act"—which opens the door enough for many

an ancient to creep in.   But limited or not, he
at least clears off a lot of moldy rubbish, and
gets further toward the truth than any of his
former colleagues.   They waste themselves
upon theories that only conceal the poet's
achievement the more, the more diligently they
are applied; he, at all events, grounds himself
upon the sound notion that there should be free
speech in art, and no protective tariffs, and no
a priori assumptions, and no testing of ideas
by mere words.   The safe ground probably lies
between the contestants, but nearer Spingarn.
The critic who really illuminates starts off much
as he starts off, but with a due regard for the
prejudices and imbecilities of the world.   I
think the best feasible practice is to be found
in certain chapters of Huneker, a critic of vastly
more solid influence and of infinitely more value
to the arts than all the prating pedagogues since
Rufus Griswold.   Here, as in the case of Poe,
a sensitive and intelligent artist re-creates the
work of other artists, but there also comes to
the ceremony a man of the world, and the
things he has to say are apposite and instructive
too.   To denounce moralizing out of hand is to
pronounce a moral judgment.   To dispute the

categories is to set up a new anti-categorical category. And to admire the work of Shakespeare is to be interested in his handling of blank verse, his social aspirations, his shot-gun marriage and his frequent concessions to the bombastic frenzy of his actors, and to have some curiosity about Mr. W. H. The really competent critic must be an empiricist. He must conduct his exploration with whatever means lie within the bounds of his personal limitation. He must produce his effects with whatever tools will work. If pills fail, he gets out his saw. If the saw won't cut, he seizes a club.

Perhaps, after all, the chief burden that lies upon Major Spingarn's theory is to be found in its label. The word "creative" is a bit too flamboyant; it says what he wants to say, but it probably says a good deal more. In this emergency, I propose getting rid of the misleading label by pasting another over it. That is, I propose the substitution of "catalytic" for "creative," despite the fact that "catalytic" is an unfamiliar word, and suggests the dog-Latin of the seminaries. I borrow it from chemistry, and its meaning is really quite simple. A catalyzer, in chemistry, is a substance that helps two other substances to react. For example, consider the case of ordinary cane sugar and water. Dissolve the sugar in the water and nothing happens. But add a few drops of acid and the sugar changes into glucose and fructose. Meanwhile, the acid itself is absolutely unchanged. All it does is to stir up the reaction between the water and the sugar. The process is called catalysis. The acid is a catalyzer.

Well, this is almost exactly the function of a genuine critic of the arts. It is his business to provoke the reaction between the work of art and the spectator. The spectator, untutored, stands unmoved; he sees the work of art, but it fails to make any intelligible impression on him; if he were spontaneously sensitive to it, there would be no need for criticism. But now comes the critic with his catalysis. He makes the work of art live for the spectator; he makes the spectator live for the work of art. Out of the process comes understanding, appreciation, intelligent enjoyment—and that is precisely what the artist tried to produce.

The Perfect Critic [1]

By T. S. ELIOT

I

> "Eriger en lois ses impressions personnelles, c'est le grand effort d'un homme s'il est sincère."—*Lettres à l'Amazone.*

COLERIDGE was perhaps the greatest of English critics, and in a sense the last. After Coleridge we have Matthew Arnold; but Arnold—I think it will be conceded—was rather a propagandist for criticism than a critic, a popularizer rather than a creator of ideas. So long as this island remains an island (and we are no nearer the Continent than were Arnold's contemporaries) the work of Arnold will be important; it is still a bridge across the Channel, and it will always have been good sense. Since Arnold's attempt to correct his countrymen, English criticism has followed two directions.

[1] From *The Sacred Wood: Essays on Poetry and Criticism*, published in 1920, and reprinted by special arrangement with Alfred A. Knopf, Inc., authorized publishers. The author has resided in England since 1913.

T. S. Eliot

When a distinguished critic observed recently, in a newspaper article, that "poetry is the most highly organized form of intellectual activity," we were conscious that we were reading neither Coleridge nor Arnold. Not only have the words "organized" and "activity," occurring together in this phrase, that familiar vague suggestion of the scientific vocabulary which is characteristic of modern writing, but one asked questions which Coleridge and Arnold would not have permitted one to ask. How is it, for instance, that poetry is more "highly organized" than astronomy, physics, or pure mathematics, which we imagine to be, in relation to the scientist who practices them, "intellectual activity" of a pretty highly organized type? "Mere strings of words," our critic continues with felicity and truth, "flung like dabs of paint across a blank canvas, may awaken surprise . . . but have no significance whatever in the history of literature." The phrases by which Arnold is best known may be inadequate, they may assemble more doubts than they dispel, but they usually have some meaning. And if a phrase like "the most highly organized form of intellectual activity"

The Perfect Critic

is the highest organization of thought of which
contemporary criticism, in a distinguished representative, is capable, then, we conclude, modern criticism is degenerate.

The verbal disease above noticed may be reserved for diagnosis by and by. It is not a
disease from which Mr. Arthur Symons (for
the quotation was, of course, not from Mr.
Symons) notably suffers. Mr. Symons represents the other tendency; he is a representative
of what is always called "esthetic criticism"
or "impressionistic criticism." And it is this
form of criticism which I propose to examine
at once. Mr. Symons, the critical successor
of Pater, and partly of Swinburne (I fancy
that the phrase "sick or sorry" is the common
property of all three), *is* the "impressionistic
critic." He, if any one, would be said to ex-
pose a sensitive and cultivated mind—cultivated, that is, by the accumulation of a considerable variety of impressions from all the
arts and several languages—before an "object"; and his criticism, if any one's, would
be said to exhibit to us, like the plate, the
faithful record of the impressions, more numerous or more refined than our own, upon a mind

T. S. Eliot

more sensitive than our own. A record, we observe, which is also an interpretation, a translation; for it must itself impose impressions upon us, and these impressions are as much created as transmitted by the criticism. I do not say at once that this is Mr. Symons; but it is the "impressionistic" critic, and the impressionistic critic is supposed to be Mr. Symons.

At hand is a volume which we may test.[1] Ten of these thirteen essays deal with single plays of Shakespeare, and it is therefore fair to take one of these ten as a specimen of the book:

> *Antony and Cleopatra* is the most wonderful, I think, of all Shakespeare's plays . . .

and Mr. Symons reflects that Cleopatra is the most wonderful of all women:

> The queen who ends the dynasty of the Ptolemies has been the star of poets, a malign star shedding baleful light, from Horace and Propertius down to Victor Hugo; and it is not to poets only . . .

[1] *Studies in Elizabethan Drama.* By Arthur Symons.

194

The Perfect Critic

What, we ask, is this for? as a page on Cleopatra, and on her possible origin in the dark lady of the Sonnets, unfolds itself. And we find, gradually, that this is not an essay on a work of art or a work of intellect; but that Mr. Symons is living through the play as one might live it through in the theater; recounting, commenting:

> In her last days Cleopatra touches a certain elevation . . . she would die a thousand times, rather than live to be a mockery and a scorn in men's mouths . . . she is a woman to the last . . . so she dies . . . the play ends with a touch of grave pity . . .

Presented in this rather unfair way, torn apart like the leaves of an artichoke, the impressions of Mr. Symons come to resemble a common type of popular literary lecture, in which the stories of plays or novels are retold, the motives of the characters set forth, and the work of art therefore made easier for the beginner. But this is not Mr. Symons' reason for writing. The reason why we find a similarity between his essay and this form of education is that *Antony and Cleopatra* is a play with which we are pretty well acquainted, and of which we have, therefore, our own impressions. We can please ourselves with our own impressions of the characters and their emotions; and we do not find the impressions of another person, however sensitive, very significant. But if we can recall the time when we were ignorant of the French symbolists, and met with *The Symbolist Movement in Literature*, we remember that book as an introduction to wholly new feelings, as a revelation. After we have read Verlaine and Laforgue and Rimbaud and return to Mr. Symons' book, we may find that our own impressions dissent from his. The book has not, perhaps, a permanent value for the one reader, but it has led to results of permanent importance for him.

The question is not whether Mr. Symons' impressions are "true" or "false." So far as you can isolate the "impression," the pure feeling, it is, of course, neither true nor false. The point is that you never rest at the pure feeling; you react in one of two ways, or, as I believe Mr. Symons does, in a mixture of the two ways. The moment you try to put the impressions into words, you either begin to analyze and construct, to "ériger en lois," or you

196

begin to create something else. It is significant that Swinburne, by whose poetry Mr. Symons may at one time have been influenced, is one man in his poetry and a different man in his criticism; to this extent and in this respect only, that he is satisfying a different impulse; he is criticizing, expounding, arranging. You may say this is not the criticism of a critic, that it is emotional, not intellectual—though of this there are two opinions, but it is in the direction of analysis and construction, a beginning to "ériger en lois," and not in the direction of creation. So I infer that Swinburne found an adequate outlet for the creative impulse in his poetry; and none of it was forced back and out through his critical prose. The style of the latter is essentially a prose style; and Mr. Symons' prose is much more like Swinburne's poetry than it is like his prose. I imagine—though here one's thought is moving in almost complete darkness—that Mr. Symons is far more disturbed, far more profoundly affected, by his reading than was Swinburne, who responded rather by a violent and immediate and comprehensive burst of admiration which may have left him internally

unchanged. The disturbance in Mr. Symons
is almost, but not quite, to the point of creating; the reading sometimes fecundates his emotions to produce something new which is not
criticism, but is not the expulsion, the ejection,
the birth of creativeness.

The type is not uncommon, although Mr.
Symons is far superior to most of the type.
Some writers are essentially of the type that
reacts in excess of the stimulus, making something new out of the impressions, but suffer
from a defect of vitality or an obscure obstruction which prevents nature from taking its
course. Their sensibility alters the object, but
never transforms it. Their reaction is that of
the ordinary emotional person developed to an
exceptional degree. For this ordinary emotional person, experiencing a work of art, has
a mixed critical and creative reaction. It is
made up of comment and opinion, and also
new emotions which are vaguely applied to
his own life. The sentimental person, in whom
a work of art arouses all sorts of emotions
which have nothing to do with that work of
art whatever, but are accidents of personal
association, is an incomplete artist. For in an

artist these suggestions made by a work of art, which are purely personal, become fused with a multitude of other suggestions from multitudinous experience, and result in the production of a new object which is no longer purely personal, because it is a work of art itself.

It would be rash to speculate, and is perhaps impossible to determine, what is unfulfilled in Mr. Symons' charming verse that overflows into his critical prose. Certainly we may say that in Swinburne's verse the circuit of impression and expression is complete; and Swinburne was therefore able, in his criticism, to be more a critic than Mr. Symons. This gives us an intimation why the artist is—each within his own limitations—oftenest to be depended upon as a critic; his criticism will be criticism, and not the satisfaction of a suppressed creative wish—which, in most other persons, is apt to interfere fatally.

Before considering what the proper critical reaction of artistic sensibility is, how far criticism is "feeling" and how far "thought," and what sort of "thought" is permitted, it may be instructive to prod a little into that other temperament, so different from Mr. Symons', which issues in generalities such as that quoted near the beginning of this article.

II

"L'écrivain de style abstrait est presque toujours un sentimental, du moins un sensitif. L'écrivain artiste n'est presque jamais un sentimental, et très rarement un sensitif."—*Le Problème du Style*.

The statement already quoted, that "poetry is the most highly organized form of intellectual activity," may be taken as a specimen of the abstract style in criticism. The confused distinction which exists in most heads between "abstract" and "concrete" is due not so much to a manifest fact of the existence of two types of mind, an abstract and a concrete, as to the existence of another type of mind, the verbal, or philosophic. I, of course, do not imply any general condemnation of philosophy; I am, for the moment, using the word "philosophic" to cover the unscientific ingredients of philosophy; to cover, in fact, the greater part of the philosophic output of the last hundred years. There are two ways in which a word may be "abstract." It may have (the word "activity," for example) a meaning which cannot be

200

grasped by appeal to any of the senses; its apprehension may require a deliberate suppression of analogies of visual or muscular experience, which is none the less an effort of imagination. "Activity" will mean for the trained scientist, if he employ the term, either nothing at all or something still more exact than anything it suggests to us. If we are allowed to accept certain remarks of Pascal and Mr. Bertrand Russell about mathematics, we believe that the mathematician deals with objects— if he will permit us to call them objects— which directly affect his sensibility. And during a good part of history the philosopher endeavored to deal with objects which he believed to be of the same exactness as the mathematician's. Finally Hegel arrived, and if not perhaps the first, he was certainly the most prodigious exponent of emotional systematization, dealing with his emotions as if they were definite objects which had aroused those emotions. His followers have as a rule taken for granted that words have definite meanings, overlooking the tendency of words to become indefinite emotions. (No one who had not witnessed the event could imagine the conviction in the tone of Professor Eucken as he pounded the table and exclaimed *Was ist Geist? Geist ist . . .*) If verbalism were confined to professional philosophers, no harm would be done. But their corruption has extended very far. Compare a medieval theologian or mystic, compare a seventeenth-century preacher, with any "liberal" sermon since Schleiermacher, and you will observe that words have changed their meanings. What they have lost is definite, and what they have gained is indefinite.

The vast accumulations of knowledge—or at least of information—deposited by the nineteenth century have been responsible for an equally vast ignorance. When there is so much to be known, when there are so many fields of knowledge in which the same words are used with different meanings, when every one knows a little about a great many things, it becomes increasingly difficult for any one to know whether he knows what he is talking about or not. And when we do not know, or when we do not know enough, we tend always to substitute emotions for thoughts. The sentence so frequently quoted in this essay will serve for an example of this process as well as any, and may be profitably contrasted with the opening phrases of the *Posterior Analytics*. Not only all knowledge, but all feeling, is in perception. The inventor of poetry as the most highly organized form of intellectual activity was not engaged in perceiving when he composed this definition; he had nothing to be aware of except his own emotion about "poetry." He was, in fact, absorbed in a very different "activity" not only from that of Mr. Symons, but from that of Aristotle.

Aristotle is a person who has suffered from the adherence of persons who must be regarded less as his disciples than as his sectaries. One must be firmly distrustful of accepting Aristotle in a canonical spirit; this is to lose the whole living force of him. He was primarily a man of not only remarkable but universal intelligence; and universal intelligence means that he could apply his intelligence to anything. The ordinary intelligence is good only for certain classes of objects; a brilliant man of science, if he is interested in poetry at all, may conceive grotesque judgments: like one poet because he reminds him of himself, or another because he expresses emotions which

T. S. Eliot

he admires; he may use art, in fact, as the outlet for the egotism which is suppressed in his own speciality. But Aristotle had none of these impure desires to satisfy; in whatever sphere of interest, he looked solely and steadfastly at the object; in his short and broken treatise he provides an eternal example—not of laws, or even of method, for there is no method except to be very intelligent, but of intelligence itself swiftly operating the analysis of sensation to the point of principle and definition.

It is far less Aristotle than Horace who has been the model for criticism up to the nineteenth century. A precept, such as Horace or Boileau gives us, is merely an unfinished analysis. It appears as a law, a rule, because it does not appear in its most general form; it is empirical. When we understand necessity, as Spinoza knew, we are free because we assent. The dogmatic critic, who lays down a rule, who affirms a value, has left his labor incomplete. Such statements may often be justifiable as a saving of time; but in matters of great importance the critic must not coerce, and he must not make judgments of worse and better.

204

The Perfect Critic

He must simply elucidate: the reader will form the correct judgment for himself.

And again, the purely "technical" critic— the critic, that is, who writes to expound some novelty or impart some lesson to practitioners of an art—can be called a critic only in a narrow sense. He may be analyzing perceptions and the means for arousing perceptions, but his aim is limited and is not the disinterested exercise of intelligence. The narrowness of the aim makes easier the detection of the merit or feebleness of the work; even of these writers there are very few—so that their "criticism" is of great importance within its limits. So much suffices for Campion. Dryden is far more disinterested; he displays much free intelligence; and yet even Dryden—or any *literary* critic of the seventeenth century—is not quite a free mind, compared, for instance, with such a mind as Rochefoucauld's. There is always a tendency to legislate rather than to inquire, to revise accepted laws, even to overturn, but to reconstruct out of the same material. And the free intelligence is that which is wholly devoted to inquiry.

Coleridge, again, whose natural abilities,

and some of whose performances, are probably more remarkable than those of any other modern critic, cannot be estimated as an intelligence completely free. The nature of the restraint in his case is quite different from that which limited the seventeenth-century critics, and is much more personal. Coleridge's metaphysical interest was quite genuine, and was, like most metaphysical interest, an affair of his emotions. But a literary critic should have no emotions except those immediately provoked by a work of art—and these (as I have already hinted) are, when valid, perhaps not to be called emotions at all. Coleridge is apt to take leave of the data of criticism, and arouse the suspicion that he has been diverted into a metaphysical hare-and-hounds. His end does not always appear to be the return to the work of art with improved perception and intensified, because more conscious, enjoyment; his center of interest changes, his feelings are impure. In the derogatory sense he is more "philosophic" than Aristotle. For everything that Aristotle says illuminates the literature which is the occasion for saying it; but Cole-

The Perfect Critic

ridge only now and then. It is one more instance of the pernicious effect of emotion.

Aristotle had what is called the scientific
mind—a mind which, as it is rarely found
among scientists except in fragments, might
better be called the intelligent mind. For
there is no other intelligence than this, and
so far as artists and men of letters are intelligent (we may doubt whether the level of
intelligence among men of letters is as high as
among men of science) their intelligence is of
this kind. Sainte-Beuve was a physiologist by
training; but it is probable that his mind, like
that of the ordinary scientific specialist, was
limited in its interest, and that this was not,
primarily, an interest in art. If he was a
critic, there is no doubt that he was a very
good one; but we may conclude that he earned
some other name. Of all modern critics, perhaps Remy de Gourmont had most of the general intelligence of Aristotle. An amateur,
though an excessively able amateur, in physiology, he combined to a remarkable degree sensitiveness, erudition, sense of fact and sense
of history, and generalizing power.

T. S. Eliot

We assume the gift of a superior sensibility. And for sensibility wide and profound reading does not mean merely a more extended pasture. There is not merely an increase of understanding, leaving the original acute impression unchanged. The new impressions modify the impressions received from the objects already known. An impression needs to be constantly refreshed by new impressions in order that it may persist at all; it needs to take its place in a system of impressions. And this system tends to become articulate in a generalized statement of literary beauty.

There are, for instance, many scattered lines and tercets in the *Divine Comedy* which are capable of transporting even a quite uninitiated reader, just sufficiently acquainted with the roots of the language to decipher the meaning, to an impression of overpowering beauty. This impression may be so deep that no subsequent study and understanding will intensify it. But at this point the impression is emotional; the reader in the ignorance which we postulate is unable to distinguish the poetry from an emotional state aroused in himself by the poetry, a state which may be merely an

The Perfect Critic

indulgence of his own emotions. The poetry may be an accidental stimulus. The end of the enjoyment of poetry is a pure contemplation from which all the accidents of personal emotion are removed; thus we aim to see the object as it really is and find a meaning for the words of Arnold. And without a labor which is largely a labor of the intelligence, we are unable to attain that stage of vision *amor intellectualis Dei*.

Such considerations, cast in this general form, may appear commonplaces. But I believe that it is always opportune to call attention to the torpid superstition that appreciation is one thing, and "intellectual" criticism something else. Appreciation in popular psychology is one faculty, and criticism another, an arid cleverness building theoretical scaffolds upon one's own perceptions or those of others. On the contrary, the true generalization is not something superposed upon an accumulation of perceptions; the perceptions do not, in a really appreciative mind, accumulate as a mass, but form themselves as a structure; and criticism is the statement in language of this structure; it is a development of sensibility. The

T. S. Eliot

bad criticism, on the other hand, is that which is nothing but an expression of emotion. And emotional people—such as stockbrokers, politicians, men of science—and a few people who pride themselves on being unemotional—detest or applaud great writers such as Spinoza or Stendhal because of their "frigidity."

The writer of the present essay once committed himself to the statement that "the poetic critic is criticizing poetry in order to create poetry." He is now inclined to believe that the "historical" and the "philosophical" critics had better be called historians and philosophers quite simply. As for the rest, there are merely various degrees of intelligence. It is fatuous to say that criticism is for the sake of "creation" or creation for the sake of criticism. It is also fatuous to assume that there are ages of criticism and ages of creativeness, as if by plunging ourselves into intellectual darkness we were in better hope of finding spiritual light. The two directions of sensibility are complementary; and as sensibility is rare, unpopular, and desirable, it is to be expected that the critic and the creative artist should frequently be the same person.

Tradition and the Individual Talent [1]

By T. S. ELIOT

I

IN English writing we seldom speak of tradition, though we occasionally apply its name in deploring its absence. We cannot refer to "the tradition" or to "a tradition"; at most, we employ the adjective in saying that the poetry of So-and-so is "traditional" or even "too traditional." Seldom, perhaps, does the word appear except in a phrase of censure. If otherwise, it is vaguely approbative, with the implication, as to the work approved, of some pleasing archeological reconstruction. You can hardly make the word agreeable to English ears without this comfortable reference to the reassuring science of archeology.

Certainly the word is not likely to appear in our appreciations of living or dead writers.

[1] From *The Sacred Wood: Essays on Poetry and Criticism*, published in 1920, and reprinted by special arrangement with Alfred A. Knopf, Inc., authorized publishers.

T. S. Eliot

Every nation, every race, has not only its own creative, but its own critical turn of mind; and is even more oblivious of the shortcomings and limitations of its critical habits than of those of its creative genius. We know, or think we know, from the enormous mass of critical writing that has appeared in the French language the critical method or habit of the French; we only conclude (we are such unconscious people) that the French are "more critical" than we, and sometimes even plume ourselves a little with the fact, as if the French were the less spontaneous. Perhaps they are; but we might remind ourselves that criticism is as inevitable as breathing, and that we should be none the worse for articulating what passes in our minds when we read a book and feel an emotion about it, for criticizing our own minds in their work of criticism. One of the facts that might come to light in this process is our tendency to insist, when we praise a poet, upon those aspects of his work in which he least resembles any one else. In these aspects or parts of his work we pretend to find what is individual, what is the peculiar essence of the man. We dwell with satisfaction upon

212

the poet's difference from his predecessors, especially his immediate predecessors; we endeavor to find something that can be isolated in order to be enjoyed. Whereas if we approach a poet without his prejudice we shall often find that not only the best, but the most individual parts of his work may be those in which the dead poets, his ancestors, assert their immortality most vigorously. And I do not mean the impressionable period of adolescence, but the period of full maturity.

Yet if the only form of tradition, of handing down, consisted in following the ways of the immediate generation before us in a blind or timid adherence to its successes, "tradition" should positively be discouraged. We have seen many such simple currents soon lost in the sand; and novelty is better than repetition. Tradition is a matter of much wider significance. It cannot be inherited, and if you want it you must obtain it by great labor. It involves, in the first place, the historical sense, which we may call nearly indispensable to any one who would continue to be a poet beyond his twenty-fifth year; and the historical sense involves a perception, not only of the pastness

213

of the past, but of its presence; the historical
sense compels a man to write not merely with
his own generation in his bones, but with a
feeling that the whole of the literature of
Europe from Homer and within it the whole
of the literature of his own country has a
simultaneous existence and composes a simultaneous order. This historical sense, which is
a sense of the timeless as well as of the temporal and of the timeless and of the temporal
together, is what makes a writer traditional.
And it is at the same time what makes a writer
most acutely conscious of his place in time, of
his contemporaneity.

No poet, no artist of any art, has his complete meaning alone. His significance, his appreciation is the appreciation of his relation to
the dead poets and artists. You cannot value
him alone; you must set him, for contrast and
comparison, among the dead. I mean this as
a principle of esthetic, not merely historical,
criticism. The necessity that he shall conform, that he shall cohere, is not one-sided;
what happens when a new work of art is created is something that happens simultaneously
to all the works of art which preceded it. The

Tradition and the Individual Talent

existing monuments form an ideal order among themselves, which is modified by the introduction of the new (the really new) work of art among them. The existing order is complete before the new work arrives; for order to persist after the supervention of novelty, the *whole* existing order must be, if ever so slightly, altered; and so the relations, proportions, values of each work of art toward the whole are readjusted; and this is conformity between the old and the new. Whoever has approved this idea of order, of the form of European, of English literature, will not find it preposterous that the past should be altered by the present as much as the present is directed by the past. And the poet who is aware of this will be aware of great difficulties and responsibilities.

In a peculiar sense he will be aware also that he must inevitably be judged by the standards of the past. I say judged, not amputated, by them; not judged to be as good as, or worse or better than, the dead; and certainly not judged by the canons of dead critics. It is a judgment, a comparison, in which two things are measured by each other. To conform

merely would be for the new work not really
to conform at all; it would not be new, and
would therefore not be a work of art. And
we do not quite say that the new is more valuable because it fits in; but its fitting in is a
test of its value—a test, it is true, which can
only be slowly and cautiously applied, for we
are none of us infallible judges of conformity. We say: it appears to conform, and is
perhaps individual, or it appears individual,
and may conform; but we are hardly likely
to find that it is one and not the other.

To proceed to a more intelligible exposition of the relation of the poet to the past:
he can neither take the past as a lump, an in-
discriminate bolus, nor can he form himself
wholly on one or two private admirations, nor
can he form himself wholly upon one preferred period. The first course is inadmissible,
the second is an important experience of youth,
and the third is a pleasant and highly desirable
supplement. The poet must be very conscious
of the main current, which does not at all flow
invariably through the most distinguished rep-
utations. He must be quite aware of the obvious fact that art never improves, but that

Tradition and the Individual Talent

the material of art is never quite the same. He must be aware that the mind of Europe —the mind of his own country—a mind which he learns in time to be much more important than his own private mind—is a mind which changes, and that this change is a development which abandons nothing *en route*, which does not superannuate either Shakespeare, or Homer, or the rock drawing of the Magdalenian draughtsmen. That this development, refinement perhaps, complication certainly, is not, from the point of view of the artist, any improvement. Perhaps not even an improvement from the point of view of the psychologist or not to the extent which we imagine; perhaps only in the end based upon a complication in economics and machinery. But the difference between the present and the past is that the conscious present is an awareness of the past in a way and to an extent which the past's awareness of itself cannot show.

Some one said: "The dead writers are remote from us because we *know* so much more than they did." Precisely, and they are that which we know.

T. S. Eliot

I am alive to a usual objection to what is clearly part of my program for the *métier* of poetry. The objection is that the doctrine requires a ridiculous amount of erudition (pedantry), a claim which can be rejected by appeal to the lives of poets in any pantheon. It will even be affirmed that much learning deadens or perverts poetic sensibility. While, however, we persist in believing that a poet ought to know as much as will not encroach upon his necessary receptivity and necessary laziness, it is not desirable to confine knowledge to whatever can be put into a useful shape for examinations, drawing-rooms, or the still more pretentious modes of publicity. Some can absorb knowledge, the more tardy must sweat for it. Shakespeare acquired more essential history from Plutarch than most men could from the whole British Museum. What is to be insisted upon is that the poet must develop or procure the consciousness of the past and that he should continue to develop this consciousness throughout his career.

What happens is a continual surrender of himself as he is at the moment to something which is more valuable. The progress of an

218

artist is a continual self-sacrifice, a continual extinction of personality.

There remains to define this process of depersonalization and its relation to the sense of tradition. It is in this depersonalization that art may be said to approach the condition of science. I shall, therefore, invite you to consider, as a suggestive analogy, the action which takes place when a bit of finely filiated platinum is introduced into a chamber containing oxygen and sulphur dioxide.

II

Honest criticism and sensitive appreciation are directed not upon the poet but upon the poetry. If we attend to the confused cries of the newspaper critics and the susurrus of popular repetition that follows, we shall hear the names of poets in great numbers; if we seek not Blue-book knowledge but the enjoyment of poetry, and ask for a poem, we shall seldom find it. In the last article I tried to point out the importance of the relation of the poem to other poems by other authors, and suggested the conception of poetry as a living

219

T. S. Eliot

whole of all the poetry that has ever been written. The other aspect of this Impersonal theory of poetry is the relation of the poem to its author. And I hinted, by an analogy, that the mind of the mature poet differs from that of the immature one not precisely in any valuation of "personality," not being necessarily more interesting, or having "more to say," but rather by being a more finely perfected medium in which special, or very varied, feelings are at liberty to enter into new combinations.

The analogy was that of the catalyst. When the two gases previously mentioned are mixed in the presence of a filament of platinum, they form sulphurous acid. This combination takes place only if the platinum is present; nevertheless the newly formed acid contains no trace of platinum, and the platinum itself is apparently unaffected; has remained inert, neutral, and unchanged. The mind of the poet is the shred of platinum. It may partly or exclusively operate upon the experience of the man himself; but, the more perfect the artist, the more completely separate in him will be the man who suffers and the

Tradition and the Individual Talent

mind which creates; the more perfectly will the mind digest and transmute the passions which are its material.

The experience, you will notice, the elements which enter the presence of the transforming catalyst, are of two kinds: emotions and feelings. The effect of a work of art upon the person who enjoys it is an experience different in kind from any experience not of art. It may be formed out of one emotion, or may be a combination of several; and various feelings, inhering for the writer in particular words or phrases or images, may be added to compose the final result. Or great poetry may be made without the direct use of any emotion whatever: composed out of feelings solely. Canto XV of the *Inferno* (Brunetto Latini) is a working up of the emotion evident in the situation; but the effect, though single as that of any work of art, is obtained by considerable complexity of detail. The last quatrain gives an image, a feeling attaching to an image, which "came," which did not develop simply out of what precedes, but which was probably in suspension in the poet's mind until the proper combination arrived for it to add itself

221

to. The poet's mind is in fact a receptacle
for seizing and storing up numberless feelings,
phrases, images, which remain there until all
the particles which can unite to form a new
compound are present together.

If you compare several representative passages of the greatest poetry you see how great
is the variety of types of combination, and
also how completely any semi-ethical criterion
of "sublimity" misses the mark. For it is not
the "greatness," the intensity, of the emotions,
the components, but the intensity of the artistic process, the pressure, so to speak, under
which the fusion takes place, that counts. The
episode of Paolo and Francesca employs a definite emotion, but the intensity of the poetry
is something quite different from whatever intensity in the supposed experience it may give
the impression of. It is no more intense, fur-
thermore, than Canto XXVI, the voyage of
Ulysses, which has not the direct dependence
upon an emotion. Great variety is possible
in the process of transmution of emotion: the
murder of Agamemnon, or the agony of
Othello, gives an artistic effect apparently
closer to a possible original than the scenes

Tradition and the Individual Talent

from Dante. In the *Agamemnon*, the artistic emotion approximates to the emotion of an actual spectator; in *Othello* to the emotion of the protagonist himself. But the difference between art and the event is always absolute; the combination which is the murder of Agamemnon is probably as complex as that which is the voyage of Ulysses. In either case there has been a fusion of elements. The ode of Keats contains a number of feelings which have nothing particular to do with the nightingale, but which the nightingale, partly, perhaps, because of its attractive name, and partly because of its reputation, served to bring together.

The point of view which I am struggling to attack is perhaps related to the metaphysical theory of the substantial unity of the soul: for my meaning is, that the poet has, not a "personality" to express, but a particular medium, which is only a medium and not a personality, in which impressions and experiences combine in peculiar and unexpected ways. Impressions and experiences which are important for the man may take no place in the poetry, and those which become important in the poetry may play quite a negligible part in the man, the personality.

I will quote a passage which is unfamiliar enough to be regarded with fresh attention in the light—or darkness—of these observations:

> And now methinks I could e'en chide myself
> For doating on her beauty, though her death
> Shall be revenged after no common action.
> Does the silkworm expend her yellow labors
> For thee? For thee does she undo herself?
> Are lordships sold to maintain ladyships
> For the poor benefit of a bewildering minute?
> Why does yon fellow falsify highways,
> And put his life between the judge's lips,
> To refine such a thing—keeps horse and men
> To beat their valors for her? . . .

In this passage (as is evident if it is taken in its context) there is a combination of positive and negative emotions: an intensely strong attraction toward beauty and an equally intense fascination by the ugliness which is contrasted with it and which destroys it. This balance of contrasted emotion is in the dramatic situation to which the speech is pertinent, but that situation alone is inadequate to it. This is, so to speak, the structural emotion, provided by the drama. But the whole effect, the dominant tone, is due to the fact that a number of floating feelings, having an affinity to this emotion by no means superficially evident, have combined with it to give us a new art emotion.

It is not in his personal emotions, the emotions provoked by particular events in his life, that the poet is in any way remarkable or interesting. His particular emotions may be simple, or crude, or flat. The emotion in his poetry will be a very complex thing, but not with the complexity of the emotions of people who have very complex or unusual emotions in life. One error, in fact, of eccentricity in poetry is to seek for new human emotions to express: and in this search for novelty in the wrong place it discovers the perverse. The business of the poet is not to find new emotions, but to use the ordinary ones and, in working them up into poetry, to express feelings which are not in actual emotions at all. And emotions which he has never experienced will serve his turn as well as those familiar to him. Consequently, we must believe that "emotion recollected in tranquillity" is an inexact formula. For it is neither emotion, nor recollection, nor, without distortion of meaning, tranquillity. It is a concentration, and a new thing resulting from the concentration, of a very great number of experiences which to the practical and active person would not seem to be experiences at all; it is a concentration which does not happen consciously or of deliberation. These experiences are not "recollected," and they finally unite in an atmosphere which is "tranquil" only in that it is a passive attending upon the event. Of course this is not quite the whole story. There is a great deal, in the writing of poetry, which must be conscious and deliberate. In fact, the bad poet is usually unconscious where he ought to be conscious, and conscious where he ought to be unconscious. Both errors tend to make him "personal." Poetry is not a turning loose of emotion, but an escape from emotion; it is not the expression of personality, but an escape from personality. But, of course, only those who have personality and emotions know what it means to want to escape from these things.

Tradition and the Individual Talent

This essay proposes to halt at the frontier
of metaphysics or mysticism, and confine itself
to such practical conclusions as can be applied
by the responsible person interested in poetry.
To divert interest from the poet to the poetry
is a laudable aim: for it would conduce to a
juster estimation of actual poetry, good and
bad. There are many people who appreciate
the expression of sincere emotion in verse, and
there is a smaller number of people who can
appreciate technical excellence. But very few
know when there is expression of *significant*
emotion, emotion which has its life in the poem
and not in the history of the poet. The emotion of art is impersonal. And the poet cannot
reach this impersonality without surrendering
himself wholly to the work to be done. And
he is not likely to know what is to be done
unless he lives in what is not merely the present, but the present moment of the past, unless
he is conscious, not of what is dead, but of
what is already living.

227

The National Genius[1]

By STUART P. SHERMAN

SOME people have one hobby and some another. Mine is studying the utterances of the
Intelligentsia—a word by which those who
think that they exhibit the latest aspect of
mind designate themselves. I like to hear what
our "young people" say, and to read what they
write; for, though they are not meek, they
will, at least in a temporal sense, inherit the
earth—and one is always interested in heirs.
So much depends upon them.

Not long ago, progressive thinkers organized
a public dinner in order to consult together
for the welfare of the Republic. The marks
of a progressive thinker are profound pessimism with regard to the past and infinite hope

[1] Originally published under this title in the *Atlantic
Monthly*, January, 1921; reprinted as the title-essay of
The Genius of America in 1923; and here reprinted by
permission of the publishers, Charles Scribner's Sons. It
is to be regretted that it has not been possible to include another essay in that volume, "The Point of View in American Criticism," in the present collection.

with regard to the future. Such a thinker was the toastmaster. Now, a thoughtful and progressive pessimist is a joy forever. He says for the rest of us those bitter things about history and society which we all feel at times, but hesitate to utter, not being so certain that we possess the antidote. I had long surmised that this was not the best possible of worlds, whether one considered it in its present drunken and reeling state, or whether one peered backward, through stratum after stratum of wrecked enterprises, into its iniquitous and catastrophic antiquity. Accordingly, I felt a kind of rich, tragic satisfaction when this toastmaster, in a ten-minute introduction, reviewed the entire history of the world from the time of the Cave Man to the time of the Treaty of Versailles, and concluded with a delightfully cheerful smile:—

"Up to date civilization has been a failure. Life is tolerable only as a preparation for a state which neither we nor our sons shall enter. We shall all die in the desert," he continued, as the gloom thickened to emit the perorational flash; "but let us die like Moses, with a look into the Promised Land."

Stuart P. Sherman

Then he began to call upon his associates in the organization of progress.

Nine-tenths of the speakers were, as is customary on such occasions, of the sort that editors include when they arrange a series of articles called "Builders of Contemporary Civilization." They were the men who get cathedrals begun, and make universities expand, legislatures vote, armies fight, money circulate, commodities exchange, and grass grow two blades for one. They spoke in a businesslike way of eliminating waste and introducing efficiency, of tapping unused resources here, of speeding up production there, of facilitating communications somewhere else. Except for the speeches of the bishop and the university president, the discourses had to my ear a somewhat mechanical twang. Yet one could not but approve and feel braced by the leading idea running through them all, which was to extend the control of man over nature and the control of a creative reason over man. All the speakers—engineer, banker, and farmer, no less than clergyman and educator—seemed to have their eyes fixed on some standard, which some internal passion for improvement urged

230

them to approximate, or to attain. I couldn't
help thinking how Franklin would have ap-
plauded the spirit of his posterity.

When, as I thought, the programme was
completed, they had substituted for the present
machinery of society a new outfit of the 1950
model, or perhaps of a still later date. The
country, under intensive cultivation, looked
like a Chinese garden. The roads, even in the
spring of the year, were not merely navigable
but Fordable. Something had happened to the
great smoke-producing cities, so that Chicago,
for instance, shone like a jewel in clear air and
sunlight. High in the heavens, innumerable
merchant vessels, guarded by aerial dread-
naughts, were passing in continuous flight
across the Gulf to South America. Production had been so enormously increased by the
increased expertness, health, and sobriety of
the producers, that a man could go to market
with only a handful of silver in his pocket
and return with bread and butter enough for
himself and his wife, and perhaps a couple of
biscuits for his dog. Every one of the teeming population, alow and aloft, male and
female, was at work in uniform, a rifle and a

wireless field-telephone within easy reach; for every one was both an expert workman and a soldier. But no one was fighting. Under the shield of that profound "preparedness," the land enjoyed uninterrupted peace and prosperity.

Perhaps I dreamed some of this. The speeches were long.

When I returned to a condition of critical consciousness, the toastmaster was introducing the last speaker as follows: "We have now provided for all matters of first-rate importance. But we have with us one of the literary leaders of the younger generation. I am going to call upon him to say a word for the way the man of the new Republic will express himself after he has been fed and clothed and housed. I shall ask him to sketch a place in our programme of democratic progress for art, music, literature, and the like—in short, for the superfluous things."

That phrase, "The superfluous things," rang in my ear like a gong: not because it was new, but because it was old; because it struck a nerve sensitive from repeated striking; because it really summed up the values of art for this

The National Genius

representative group of builders; because it
linked itself up with a series of popularly contrasted terms—practical and liberal studies,
business English and literary English, useful
and ornamental arts, valuable and graceful
accomplishments, necessaries and luxuries of
life, chemists and professors of English, and
so on *ad infinitum*. I myself was a professor
of superfluous things, and therefore, a superfluous professor. As I turned this uncomfort-
able thought over in my mind, it occurred to
me that things are superfluous only with reference to particular ends; and that, in a comprehensive plan of preparation for a satisfac-
tory national life, we might be compelled to
revise the epithets conventionally applied to
the arts which express our craving for beauty,
harmony, happiness.

Before I had gone far in this train of
thought, the literary artist was addressing the
business men. His discourse was so remarkable, and yet so representative of our most conspicuous group of "young people," that I reproduce the substance of it here.

"The young men of my generation," he began, "propose the emancipation of the arts in

Stuart P. Sherman

America. Before our time, such third-rate talents as the country produced were infected, by our institutions, and by the multitude, with a sense of their Messianic mission. Dominated by the twin incubi of Puritanism and Democracy, they servilely associated themselves with political, moral, and social programmes, and made beauty a prostitute to utility. Our generation of artists has seen through all the solemn humbug of your plans for the 'welfare of the Republic.' With a clearer-eyed pessimism than that of our toastmaster, we have not merely envisaged the failure of civilization in the past: we have also foreseen its failure in the future.

"We have talked with wiser counselors than those pious Philistines, our naïve Revolutionary Fathers. George Moore, our great contemporary, tells us that 'Humanity is a pigsty, where liars, hypocrites, and the obscene in spirit congregate: and it has been so since the great Jew conceived it, and it will be so till the end.' Leopardi, who in this respect was our pioneer, declares that 'all things else being vain, disgust of life represents all that

234

is substantial and real in the life of man.'
Theodore Dreiser, our profound philosophical
novelist, views the matter, however, with a
bit of creative hopefulness. Though God, as
he has assured us, cares nothing for the pure
in heart, yet God does offer a 'universe-eating .
career to the giant,' recking not how the life-
force manifests itself, 'so long as it achieves
avid, forceful, artistic expression.' From serving the middle-class American, Flaubert frees
us, saying, 'Hatred of the bourgeois is the
beginning of virtue.' Mr. Spingarn, our
learned theorist, brushes away the critical cob-
webs of antique poetic doctrine, and gives us
a clean esthetic basis, by his revelation that
'beauty aims neither at morals nor at truth';
and that 'it is not the purpose of poetry to
further the cause of democracy, or any other
practical "cause," any more than it is the purpose of bridge-building to further the cause
of Esperanto.' We have had to import our
philosophy in fragments from beyond the bor-
ders of Anglo-Saxonia, and we have had to
call in the quick Semitic intelligence to piece it
together. But here it is; and you will recog-

nize that it liberates us from Puritanism and from Democracy. It emancipates us from you!

"You ask me, perhaps," continued the young representative of American letters, "what we intend to do with this new freedom, which, as Mr. Ludwig Lewisohn truly says, is our 'central passion.' Well, we intend *to let ourselves out*. If you press me as to what I mean by that, I can refer you to the new psychology. This invaluable science, developed by great German investigators, has recently announced, as you possibly know, an epoch-making discovery—namely, that most of the evil in the world is due to self-control. To modern inquiry, it appears that what all the moralists, especially in Anglo-Saxon countries, have tried to curb or to suppress is precisely what they should have striven to release. If you wish corroboration, let me quote the words of our talented English colleague, Mr. W. L. George, the novelist, who says, 'I suspect that it does a people no good if its preoccupations find no outlet.'

"In passing I will remark that Mr. George, being an Englishman, shows a certain taint of inherited English Puritanism in defending letting the people out *in order to do them good*. From the point of view of the new philosophy, letting one's self out completely and perfectly is art, which has no purpose and therefore requires no defense.

"But to return: what are the 'preoccupations' of the ordinary man? Once more Mr. George shall answer for us. 'A large proportion of his thoughts run on sex if he is a live man.' French literature proves the point abundantly; American literature, as yet, very imperfectly and scantily. Consequently, a young American desiring to enlarge his sex-consciousness must import his fiction from overseas. But our own Mr. Cabell has also begun to prove the point as well as a foreigner. His release of the suppressed life is very precious. If he were encouraged, instead of being nipped by the frost of a Puritanical censorship; if a taste were developed to support him, he might do for us what George Moore is trying, subterraneously, to do for England.

"Our own Mr. Dreiser has been so preoccupied with this subject that he has been obliged to neglect a little his logic and his grammar. His thinking, however, runs none the less surefootedly to the conclusion reached by Mr. George. What does that remorseless artist-thinker, Mr. Dreiser, say? He says: 'It is the desire to enthrone and enhance, by every possible detail of ornamentation, comfort, and color,—love, sensual gratification,—that man in the main moves, and by that alone.' We do not maintain that Mr. Dreiser is a flawless writer. But if, at your leisure, you will study that sentence from his latest and ripest book, till you discover its subject, predicate, and object, and can bridge its anacoluthon, and reconcile 'in the main' with 'by that alone,' then you will be in a position to grasp our leading idea for the future of the arts in America."

When the young man resumed his seat, there was a ripple of applause among the ladies, one of whom told me later that she thought the speaker's voice "delicious" and his eyes "soulful." But I noticed that the bishop was purple with suppressed wrath; that the university president had withdrawn; while the other builders of civilization, notably the business men, were nodding with a kind of patient and puzzled resignation.

In my neighborhood there was a quick little buzz of questions: "Will you tell me what all that has to do with a program of democratic progress?"—"What is George Moore trying subterraneously to do for England? Is he interested in the collieries? I thought he was a novelist."—"He has downright insulted them," said my neighbor on the right, "don't you think?"

"Why, no," I replied, "not exactly. He was asked to speak on the superfluous things; and he has really demonstrated that they are superfluous. After this, don't you see, the builders of civilization can go on with their work and not worry about the arts. He has told them that beauty is not for them; and they will swiftly conclude that they are not for beauty. I think he has very honestly expressed what our radical young people are thinking. They are in revolt. They wish by all means to widen the traditional breach between the artist and the Puritan."

"What do you mean by Puritan?" inquired

my friend, as we made our way out of the hall together.

He is a simple-hearted old gentleman who doesn't follow the new literature, but still reads Hawthorne and George Eliot.

"It isn't," I explained, "what I mean by Puritan that signifies. It is what the young people mean. A Puritan for them is any man who believes it possible to distinguish between good and evil, and who also believes that, having made the distinction, his welfare depends upon his furthering the one and curbing the other."

"But," cried the old gentleman in some heat, "in that sense, we are all Puritans. That isn't theological Puritanism. That is scarcely even moral Puritanism. It's just—it's just ordinary horse sense. In that sense, for God's sake, who isn't a Puritan?"

I recalled an old case that I thought would illustrate the present situation. "There was Judge Keeling," I said, "in Charles the Second's time. Judge Keeling put Bunyan in jail for failing to use the Book of Common Prayer, and similar misdemeanors. In the reign of the same Defender of the Faith, two

240

merry wits and poets of his court became flown with wine and, stripping themselves naked, ran through the streets, giving a healthy outlet to their suppressed selves in songs of a certain sort. The constable, an ordinary English Puritan, so far misunderstood the spiritual autonomy which the artist should enjoy, that he arrested the two liberators of art. When, however, the news reached Judge Keeling, he released the young men and laid the constable by the heels; which, as Pepys,—himself a patron of the arts, yet a bit of a Puritan,— as Pepys remarked, was a 'horrid shame.' Now Judge Keeling, I think our own young people would admit, was not a Puritan, even in the latest sense of the term."

"But those Restoration fellows," replied my friend,—"Keeling and the wits and the rest of them,—they were opposing the sense of the whole English nation. They made no headway. No one took them seriously. They all disappeared like gnats in a snowstorm. When the central current of English life had done its scouring work, people thought of your two poets as mere stable-boys of the Restoration. Surely you don't think our democratic young people are so silly as to imitate them? We have no merry monarch to reward them. What do they gain by setting themselves against the common sense?"

"Notoriety," I said, "which is as sweet under a republican as under a monarchical form of government. I used to think that to insult the common sense and always to be speaking contemptuously of the 'bourgeoisie,' implied sycophancy, either to a corrupt and degenerate aristocracy, or to a peculiarly arrogant and atheistical lowest class. But our 'democratic young people,' as you call them, preserve and foster this artistic snobbishness as a form of self-expression.

"When Mr. Dreiser declares that God cares nothing for the Ten Commandments or for the pure in heart, he really means that inanimate nature cares nothing for them, and that the animal kingdom and he and the heroes of his books follow nature. But he denies a faith which, in some fifty millions of native Americans survives the decay of dogma, and somehow in attenuated form, keeps the country from going wholly to the dogs. For, of course, if it were demonstrable that God had abandoned a charge so important, plain men of sense would quietly assume responsibility and 'carry on' in his stead."

"I quite agree with you," said the old gentleman; "but as I am not acquainted with the author you mention and am just completing my third reading of *Middlemarch*, I will turn in here. Good-night."

I went on down the street, resuming, unaccompanied, the more difficult part of my meditation on the place of the fine arts in a programme of democratic progress, and internally debating with the young man who had caused such a sensation at dinner. Having made this general acknowledgment of his inspiration, I shall not attempt to reproduce our dialogue; for I found that he simply repeated the main points of his speech, and interrupted my comment upon it.

When Mr. Spingarn, who, as a man, is concerned with truth, morals, and democracy, and has a personal record of civil and military service—when Mr. Spingarn, as an esthetic theorist, declares that beauty is not concerned with truth or morals or democracy, he makes a philosophical distinction which I have no doubt that Charles the Second would have understood, approved, and could, at need, have illustrated. But he says what the American schoolboy knows to be false to the history of beauty in this country. By divorcing, in his super-subtle Italian fashion, form from substance, he has separated beauty from her traditional associates in American letters, and so has left her open to seduction.

Beauty, whether we like it or not, has a heart full of service. Emancipated, she will still be seeking some vital activity. You have heard how the new writers propose to employ her new leisure: in extending the ordinary man's preoccupation with sex. We don't, you will observe, by the emancipation of the arts from service to truth, morals, and democracy —we don't obtain a "disinterested" beauty. We obtain merely a beauty with different interests—serving "sensual gratification" and propagating the curiously related doctrine that God cares nothing for the Ten Commandments or for the pure in heart.

We arrive finally at some such comprehensive formulation of relationships as this: It is the main function of art to deny what it is the

244

main function of truth, morals, and democracy
to affirm. Our speaker for the younger generation has made all this so clear that I suspect the bishop is going home resolved to take
music out of his churches. The university
president is perhaps deciding to replace his
professor of Italian painting by an additional
professor of soil-fertility. As for the captains
of industry, they can hardly be blamed if they
mutter among themselves: "May the devil fly
away with the fine arts! Let's get back to
business."

It is to be hoped, nevertheless, that the devil
will not fly away with the fine arts or the fine
artists, or with our freshly foot-loose and wan-
dering beauty; for the builders of civilization
have need of them. If the young people were
not misled by more or less alien-spirited guides,
the national genius itself would lead them into
a larger life.

When our forefathers, whom it is now customary to speak of as "grim," outlined their
programme for a new republic, though they had
many more immediately pressing matters on
their minds, they included among objects to be
safeguarded, indeed, among the inalienable

rights of mankind, "the pursuit of happiness."
It appears that they, like ourselves, had some
dim idea that the ultimate end of their preparation was, not to fight the English or the
savages or the wilderness, but to enjoy, they
or their posterity, some hitherto unexperienced
felicity. That, at heart, was what sustained
them under the burdens and heats of a pioneering civilization, through those years when they
dispensed with such ingredients of happiness
as musical comedy and moving pictures, and
when the most notable piece of imagist verse
was Franklin's proverb, "It is hard for an
empty sack to stand upright"—a one-line poem
of humor, morality, insight, and imagination
all compact.

We, too, entertain, we ordinary puritanical
Americans, some shadowy notions of a time,
when, at more frequent intervals than now,
men shall draw in a delighted breath and cry,
"Oh, that this moment might endure forever!"
We believe in this far-off time, because, at
least once or twice in a lifetime, each of us
experiences such a moment, or, feeling the wind
of its retreating wing, knows that it has just
gone by. It may have been in the spell-bound

glow of some magical sunset, or at the sound
of a solemn music, or in the sudden apprehension of a long-sought truth, or at the thrill and
tightening of resolution in some crisis, or in
the presence of some fair marble image of a
thought that keeps its beauty and serenity
while we fret and fade. It may even have
been at some vision, seen in the multitude of
business, of a new republic revealed to the traveling imagination, like a shining city set on a
hill in the flash of a midnight storm. Till life
itself yields such moments less charily, it is
incumbent upon the artist to send them as
often as he can.

There came among us in war time an English poet whose face was as sad as his who
from the Judecca climbed to see again *delle
cose belle che porta il ciel*—the sky-borne
beauty of the stars. He had been where his
countrymen, fighting with incredible heroism,
had suffered one of the most heart-breaking
and bloody defeats in English history. His
memory was seared with remembrance of the
filth, waste, wounds, and screaming lunacy
of the battle-front to which he was about to
return. When some one asked him to write

his name in a volume of his poems, he inscribed
below it this line of his own verse:—

The days that make us happy make us wise.

Why these days? Because in them we learn
the final object of all our preparation. These
days serve us as measures of the success of our
civilization.

The ultimate reason for including the
"superfluous things"—art, music, literature—
in a plan of national preparation is that,
rightly used, they are both causes and consequences of happiness. They are the seed and
the fruit of that fine and gracious and finished
national life towards which we aspire. When
the body is fed and sheltered, there remain to
be satisfied—as what Puritan does not know?
—the inarticulate hungers of the heart, to
which all the arts are merely some of the ministers. Other ministers are religion, morality,
patriotism, science, truth. It is only by har-
monious coöperation that they can ever hope
to satisfy the whole heart, the modern heart,
with its ever-widening range of wakened hungers. It is certainly not by banishing or ignoring the austerer ministers, and making

poetry, painting, and music perform a Franco-Turkish dance of sensual invitation—it is not thus that the artist should expect to satisfy a heart as religious, as moral, and as democratic as the American heart is, by its bitterest critics, declared to be.

"Art is expression," says the learned theorist of the young people, "and poets succeed or fail by their success or failure in completely expressing themselves." Let us concede that the poet who expresses completely what is in him by a hymn to the devil is as perfect an artist as a poet who expresses what is in him by the Iliad. Then let us remark that the poet who hymns the devil, the devil is likely to fly away with. And let us add as rapidly as possible a little series of neglected truisms. An artist is a man living in society. A great artist is a great man living in a great society. When a great artist expresses himself completely, it is found invariably that he has expressed, not merely himself, but also the dominant thought and feeling of the men with whom he lives. Mr. Spingarn, indeed, indirectly admits the point when he says: "If the ideals they [the poets] express are not the ideals we admire most, we must blame, not the poets, but ourselves; in the world where morals count, *we have failed to give them the proper materials out of which to rear a nobler edifice.*" (Italics mine.) This seems to mean that society is responsible for the artist, even if the artist is not responsible to society. Society gives him, as a man, what, as an artist, he expresses.

I have perhaps hinted here and elsewhere my suspicion that Mr. Dreiser, a capital illustrative example, is not a great novelist, because, though living in a great society, he does not express or represent its human characteristics, but confines himself to an exhibition of the habits and traits of animals. Is it that we have not given him materials to rear a nobler edifice? That which we—that is, society—can give to a novelist is the molding and formative influence of the national temper and character. What have we given to Mr. Dreiser? What, in short, are the dominant traits of the national genius? I am delighted to discover in Mr. Dreiser's latest book that he himself knows pretty well what the national genius is, how it has manifested itself in religion and politics, and how it is nourished

and sustained by ancient traditions and strong
racial proclivities. I like to agree with our
young people when I can. When I find one
of them testifying, contrary to their custom,
that America does now possess a powerful
national culture, I like to applaud his discern-
ment. It is a pleasure to make amends for
my disparagement of Mr. Dreiser as a novelist, by illustrating his critical ability with
these words of his on the national genius:—

"No country in the world (at least, none
that I know anything about) has such a peculiar, such a seemingly fierce determination to
make the Ten Commandments work. It would
be amusing, if it were not pitiful, their faith
in these binding religious ideals. I have never
been able to make up my mind whether this
springs from the zealotry of the Puritans who
landed at Plymouth Rock, or whether it is
rooted in the soil . . . or whether it is a product of the Federal Constitution, compounded
by such idealists as Paine and Jefferson and
Franklin and the more or less religious and
political dreamers of the preconstitutional
days. *Certain it is that no such profound
moral idealism animated the French in Can-*

ada, the Dutch in New York, the Swedes in New Jersey, or the mixed French and English in the extreme South and New Orleans." (Italics mine.)

I know how differently our young people feel; but, to my thinking, a national genius animated by an incomparably profound moral idealism does not seem such a contemptible molding and formative influence for an artist to undergo. English-speaking poets, from Spenser to Walt Whitman, have grown great under the influence of such an environing spirit. At any rate, if the great artist, in expressing himself, expresses also the society of which he is a part, it should seem to follow, like a conclusion in geometry, that a great American artist must express the "profound moral idealism" of America. To rail against it, to lead an insurrection against it, is to repeat the folly of the Restoration wits. If in this connection one may use a bit of the American language, it is to "buck" the national genius; and this is an enterprise comparable with bucking a stone wall. On the other hand to acknowledge the leadership of the national genius, to subject one's self to its influence, to serve it ac-

The National Genius

cording to one's talents, to find beautiful and potent forms to express its working—this is to ally one's self with the general creative effort of the country in all fields of activity; this is to be in a benign conspiracy with one's time and place, and to be upborne by the central stream of tendency.

There is small place for Bohemia in democratic art. I sometimes wonder with what spiritual refugees, under what rafters, those poets and novelists live who are so anxious to secede from the major effort of their countrymen. For their own sakes one wishes that they might cultivate acquaintance with our eminent "builders of civilization." The good that I should expect from this contact is a vision of the national life, a sense of the national will, which are usually possessed in some degree by those Americans, whatever their esthetic deficiencies, who bear the burden of the state, or are widely conversant with its business, or preside over its religious, moral, or educational undertakings. I do not intend in the least to suggest that the artist should become propagandist or reformer, or that he should go to the bishop or the statesman for

Stuart P. Sherman

a commission, though I believe that Leonardo and Michael Angelo did some very tolerable things under direct inspiration of that nature. What one feels is rather that intercourse with such men might finally create in our artistic secessionists a consciousness of the ignobility of their aims. For in America it will be found more and more that the artist who does not in some fashion concern himself with truth, morals, and democracy, is unimportant, is ignoble.

In an unfinished world, where religion has become so largely a matter of traditional sentiments and observances, poetry has a work to do, poetry of any high seriousness. Our critics and poets of vision have long since recognized what that work is. "I said to Bryant and to these young people," wrote Emerson in his journal many years ago, "that the high poetry of the world from the beginning has been ethical, and it is the tendency of the ripe modern mind to produce it."—"I hate literature," said Whitman, perhaps over-emphatically expressing the traditional American disdain for art in its merely decorative and recreative aspects. "Literature is big only in one

254

The National Genius

way, when used as an aid in the growth of the
humanities." Our young people, of course,
will exclaim that these are typical utterances
of our New England Puritanism, fatal to the
arts; but, as a matter of fact, this Puritanism
is of a sort that the New Englanders shared
with Plato and Aristotle, who have not been
fatal to the arts. When Emerson said,
"Honor every truth by use," he expressed, I
think, what Socrates would have approved,
and at the same time he spoke in fullest accord
with the national genius, ever driving at practice, ever pressing towards the fulfillment of
its vision.

Why should a spokesman for *belles-lettres*,
bred in the national tradition, hesitate to go
before a group of "practical" men and talk to
them, unashamed, of the "utilities" of artistic
expression? He may borrow a figure from
the economist, and declare that the poet "so-
cializes" the spiritual wealth of the country.
Art is rooted in social instinct, in a desire to
communicate goods to others, to share one's
private experience and anticipations. It is the
spontaneous overflow of thoughts and feelings
which one cannot consume alone. "Full of

the common joy," says Donne, "I uttered some." This is your true and unassailable communism. When Saint Gaudens, having conceived his heroic and inspiring image of Colonel Shaw leading his colored troops, sets it up on Boston Common, it becomes common property; and the loafer in the park, the student, the hurrying merchant, the newsboy, are equal sharers in its commemoration and inspiration. A village poet with an ethical bent makes this thought sing:—

> When duty whispers low, "Thou must,"
> The youth replies, "I can,"—

and he has slipped a spiritual gold-piece into the palm of each of his fellow countrymen. This is wealth really distributed. It would be of advantage to both bards and business men if some spiritual economist would remind them more frequently that the wealth of a community is in proportion to the number of such ideas that it has in common.

Among builders of American civilization, many means are now discussed for awakening national pride and attaching the affections of the people to the state; conspicuous among

The National Genius

them are, or were, Liberty Bonds, nationalization of the railroads, and universal military service. Robert Burns and Sir Walter did the work more simply and cheaply for Scotland. It has never been hard for the native-born American to hold America "first" in political affairs; but musicians as such, painters as such, men of letters as such, cannot, without straining the meaning of the word, hold her first till her national genius expresses itself as adequately, as nobly, in music, painting, and literature, as it has, on the whole, in the great political crises. Irving, at the beginning of the last century, worked with a clear understanding of our deficiencies when he wrote his *Rip Van Winkle* and other legends of the Hudson Valley, with the avowed purpose "to clothe home scenes and places and familiar names with those imaginative and whimsical associations so seldom met with in our new country, but which live like charms and spells about the cities of the Old World, binding the heart of the native inhabitant to his home."

You may persuade all men to buy Liberty Bonds or to invest in the stock of nationalized railroads, or you may legislate them into the army; but you cannot dragoon them into crying, "O beautiful, my country!" That is the work of the poets, who have entwined their loyalty with their heart-strings. That is the work of the artists, who have made their Americanism vital, devout, affectionate. "How can our love increase," asks Thoreau, "unless our loveliness increases also?" A good question for "Americanizers" to meditate upon. It would benefit both public men and artists if some one reminded them more frequently that one of the really important tasks of national preparation is to draw out and express in forms of appealing beauty, audible as poetry or music, visible as painting or sculpture, the purpose and meaning of this vast half-articulate land, so that our hosts of new and unlearned citizens may come to understand her as they understand the divine compassion—by often kneeling before some shrine of the Virgin.

When art becomes thus informed with the larger life of the country, it vitalizes and gives permanency to the national ideals. It transmits the hope and courage and aspiration of one generation to the next, with the emotional

glow and color undiminished and unimpaired.
If we receive and cherish the tradition, our
imaginative experience transcends the span of
our natural lives. We live in the presence, as
Burke declared, of our "canonized" forefathers
and in a kind of reverent apprehension of our
posterity, happily conscious of a noble and
distinguished national thought and feeling,
"above the vulgar practice of the hour."

Precisely because Lincoln had communed
intimately with the national genius and obeyed
devoutly its promptings, America ceases, in
some passages of his letters and speeches, to be
a body politic and becomes a living soul. Who
was it wrote that letter to Mrs. Bixby on the
loss of her five sons in battle? "I cannot re-
frain from tendering to you the consolation
that may be found in the thanks of the Republic that they died to save. I pray that our
Heavenly Father may assuage the anguish of
your bereavement, and leave you only the cherished memory of the loved and lost, and the
solemn pride that must be yours to have laid
so costly a sacrifice upon the altar of freedom."

The words are thrilling still with the pathos
and splendor of patriotic death. They seem

charged with the tears and valor of the whole Civil War. To speak like that of death is to unfold the meaning of the Latin verse: *Dulce et decorum est pro patria mori*. It is to hallow the altar on which the sacrifice is made. One can hardly read the letter through with dry eyes; and yet reading it makes one very happy. It makes one happy because it renders one in imagination a sharer of that splendid sacrifice, that solemn pride, that divine consolation. It makes one happy because it uplifts the heart and purges it of private interests, and admits one into the higher, and more spacious, and grander life of the nation. For my purposes I am not writing an anti-climax when I say that it makes one happy because it is the perfect expression of a deep, grave, and noble emotion, which is the supreme triumph of the expressive arts. It is the work of a great artist. Was it Lincoln? Or was it the America of our dreams? It was the voice of the true emancipator of our art, who will always understand that his task is not to set Beauty and Puritanism at loggerheads, but to make Puritanism beautiful.

For Wed.
Sept 20

Footnote on Criticism [1]

By H. L. MENCKEN

NEARLY all the discussions of criticism that I
am acquainted with start off with a false assumption, to wit, that the primary motive of
the critic, the impulse which makes a critic of
him instead of, say, a politician, or a stock-
broker, is pedagogical—that he writes because
he is possessed by a passion to advance the en-
lightenment, to put down error and wrong, to
disseminate some specific doctrine: psychological, epistemological, historical, or esthetic.
This is true, it seems to me, only of bad critics,
and its degree of truth increases in direct ratio
to their badness. The motive of the critic who
is really worth reading—the only critic of
whom, indeed, it may be said truthfully that
it is at all possible to read him, save as an act
of mental discipline—is something quite dif-

[1] Originally published in the *New Republic* in 1921;
reprinted in 1922 in *Prejudices, Third Series*, and here reprinted by special arrangement with Alfred A. Knopf, Inc.,
authorized publishers.

H. L. Mencken

ferent. That motive is not the motive of the pedagogue, but the motive of the artist. It is no more and no less than the simple desire to function freely and beautifully, to give outward and objective form to ideas that bubble inwardly and have a fascinating lure in them, to get rid of them dramatically and make an articulate noise in the world. It was for this reason that Plato wrote the *Republic*, and for this reason that Beethoven wrote the Ninth Symphony, and it is for this reason, to drop a million miles, that I am writing the present essay. Everything else is afterthought, mock-modesty, messianic delusion—in brief, affectation and folly. Is the contrary conception of criticism widely cherished? Is it almost universally held that the thing is a brother to jurisprudence, advertising, laparotomy, chautauqua lecturing and the art of the schoolmarm? Then certainly the fact that it is so held should be sufficient to set up an overwhelming probability of its lack of truth and sense. If I speak with some heat, it is as one who has suffered. When, years ago, I devoted myself diligently to critical pieces upon the writings of Theodore Dreiser, I found that

Footnote on Criticism

practically every one who took any notice of my proceedings at all fell into either one of two assumptions about my underlying purpose: (*a*) that I had a fanatical devotion for Mr. Dreiser's ideas and desired to propagate them, or (*b*) that I was an ardent patriot, and yearned to lift up American literature. Both assumptions were false. I had then, and I have now, very little interest in many of Mr. Dreiser's main ideas; when we meet, in fact, we usually quarrel about them. And I am wholly devoid of public spirit, and haven't the least lust to improve American literature; if it ever came to what I regard as perfection my job would be gone. What, then, was my motive in writing about Mr. Dreiser so copiously? My motive, well known to Mr. Dreiser himself and to every one else who knew me as intimately as he did, was simply and solely to sort out and give coherence to the ideas of Mr. Mencken, and to put them into suave and ingratiating terms, and to discharge them with a flourish, and maybe with a phrase of pretty song, into the dense fog that blanketed the Republic.

The critic's choice of criticism rather than

of what is called creative writing is chiefly a matter of temperament—perhaps, more accurately of hormones—with accidents of education and environment to help. The feelings that happen to be dominant in him at the moment the scribbling frenzy seizes him are feelings inspired, not directly by life itself, but by books, pictures, music, sculpture, architecture, religion, philosophy—in brief, by some other man's feelings about life. They are thus, in a sense, secondhand, and it is no wonder that creative artists so easily fall into the theory that they are also second-rate. Perhaps they usually are. If, indeed, the critic continues on this plane—if he lacks the intellectual agility and enterprise needed to make the leap from the work of art to the vast and mysterious complex of phenomena behind it—then they *always* are, and he remains no more than a fugleman or policeman to his betters. But if a genuine artist is concealed within him— if his feelings are in any sense profound and original, and his capacity for self-expression is above the average of educated men—then he moves inevitably from the work of art to life itself, and begins to take on a dignity that

he formerly lacked. It is impossible to think
of a man of any actual force and originality,
universally recognized as having those qualities, who spent his whole life appraising and
describing the work of other men. Did Goethe,
or Carlyle, or Matthew Arnold, or Sainte-
Beuve, or Macaulay, or even, to come down
a few pegs, Lewes, or Lowell, or Hazlitt?
Certainly not. The thing that becomes most
obvious about the writings of all such men,
once they are examined carefully, is that the
critic is always being swallowed up by the creative artist—that what starts out as the review of a book, or a play, or other work of
art, usually develops very quickly into an independent essay upon the theme of that work
of art, or upon some theme that it suggests—
in a word, that it becomes a fresh work of
art, and only indirectly related to the one that
suggested it. This fact, indeed, is so plain
that it scarcely needs statement. What the
pedagogues always object to in, for example,
the *Quarterly* reviewers is that they forgot the
books they were supposed to review, and wrote
long papers—often, in fact, small books—expounding ideas suggested (or not suggested)

# H. L. Mencken

by the books under review. Every critic who
is worth reading falls inevitably into the same
habit. He cannot stick to his task: what is before him is always infinitely less interesting to
him than what is within him. If he is genu-
inely first-rate—if what is within him stands
the test of type, and wins an audience, and
produces the reactions that every artist craves
—then he usually ends by abadoning the criticism of specific works of art altogether, and
setting up shop as a general merchant in general ideas, *i.e.*, as an artist working in the
materials of life itself.

Mere reviewing, however conscientiously
and competently it is done, is plainly a much
inferior business. Like writing poetry, it is
chiefly a function of intellectual immaturity.
The young literatus just out of the university,
having as yet no capacity for grappling with
the fundamental mysteries of existence, is put
to writing reviews of books, or plays, or music,
or painting. Very often he does it extremely
well; it is, in fact, not hard to do well, for
even decayed pedagogues often do it, as such
graves of the intellect as the New York *Times*
bear witness. But if he continues to do it,

266

Footnote on Criticism

whether well or ill, it is a sign to all the world
that his growth ceased when they made him
Artium Baccalaureus. Gradually he becomes,
whether in or out of the academic grove, a
professor, which is to say, a man devoted to
diluting and retailing the ideas of his superiors
—not an artist, not even a bad artist, but almost the antithesis of an artist. He is learned,
he is sober, he is painstaking and accurate—
but he is as hollow as a jug. Nothing is in
him save the ghostly echoes of other men's
thoughts and feelings. If he were a genuine
artist he would have thoughts and feelings of
his own, and the impulse to give them objective form would be irresistible. An artist can
no more withstand that impulse than a politician can withstand the temptations of a job.
There are no mute, inglorious Miltons, save
in the hallucinations of poets. The one sound
test of a Milton is that he functions as a Milton. His difference from other men lies precisely in the superior vigor of his impulse to
self-expression, not in the superior beauty and
loftiness of his ideas. Other men, in point of
fact, often have the same ideas, or perhaps
even loftier ones, but they are able to suppress

them, usually on grounds of decorum, and so
they escape being artists, and are respected by
right-thinking persons, and die with money in
the bank, and are forgotten in two weeks.

Obviously, the critic whose performance we
are commonly called upon to investigate is a
man standing somewhere along the path leading from the beginning that I have described
to the goal. He has got beyond being a mere
cataloguer and valuer of other men's ideas, but
he has not yet become an autonomous artist
—he is not yet ready to challenge attention
with his own ideas alone. But it is plain that
his motion, in so far as he is moving at all,
must be in the direction of that autonomy—
that is, unless one imagines him sliding backward into senile infantilism: a spectacle not
unknown to literary pathology, but too pa-
thetic to be discussed here. Bear this motion
in mind, and the true nature of his aims and
purposes becomes clear; more, the incurable
falsity of the aims and purposes usually cred-
ited to him becomes equally clear. He is not
actually trying to perform an impossible act
of arctic justice upon the artist whose work
gives him a text. He is not trying with math-

Footnote on Criticism

ematical passion to find out exactly what was in that artist's mind at the moment of creation, and to display it precisely and in an ecstasy of appreciation. He is not trying to bring the work discussed into accord with some transient theory of esthetics, or ethics, or truth, or to determine its degree of departure from that theory. He is not trying to lift up the fine arts, or to defend democracy against sense, or to promote happiness at the domestic hearth, or to convert sophomores into right-thinkers, or to serve God. He is not trying to fit a group of novel phenomena into the orderly process of history. He is not even trying to discharge the catalytic office that I myself, in a romantic moment, once sought to force upon him. He is, first and last, simply trying to express himself. He is trying to arrest and challenge a sufficient body of readers, to make them pay attention to him, to impress them with the charm and novelty of his ideas, to provoke them into an agreeable (or shocked) awareness of him, and he is trying to achieve thereby for his own inner ego the grateful feeling of a function performed, a tension relieved, a *katharsis* attained which Wagner achieved when he wrote "Die Walküre," and a hen achieves every time she lays an egg.

Joseph Conrad is moved by that necessity to write romances; Bach was moved to write music; poets are moved to write poetry; critics are moved to write criticism. The form is nothing; the only important thing is the motive power, and it is the same in all cases. It is the pressing yearning of every man who has ideas in him to empty them upon the world, to hammer them into plausible and ingratiating shapes, to compel the attention and respect of his equals, to lord it over his inferiors. So seen, the critic becomes a far more transparent and agreeable fellow than ever he was in the discourses of the psychologists who sought to make him a mere appraiser in an intellectual customs house, a gauger in a distillery of the spirit, a just and infallible judge upon the cosmic bench. Such offices, in point of fact, never fit him. He always bulges over their confines. So labeled and estimated, it inevitably turns out that the specific critic under examination is a very bad one, or no critic at all. But when he is thought of, not as pedagogue, but as artist, then he begins to take

Footnote on Criticism

on reality, and, what is more, dignity. Carlyle was surely no just and infallible judge; on the contrary, he was full of prejudices, biles, naïvetés, humors. Yet he is read, consulted, attended to. Macaulay was unfair, inaccurate, fanciful, lyrical—yet his essays live. Arnold had his faults too, and so did Sainte-Beuve, and so did Goethe, and so did many another of that line—and yet they are remembered to-day, and all the learned and conscientious critics of their time, laboriously concerned with the precise intent of the artists under review, and passionately determined to set it forth with god-like care and to relate it exactly to this or that great stream of ideas— all these pedants are forgotten. What saved Carlyle, Macaulay and company is as plain as day. They were first-rate artists. They could make the thing charming, and that is always a million times more important than making it true.

Truth, indeed, is something that is believed in completely only by persons who have never tried personally to pursue it to its fastnesses and grab it by the tail. It is the adoration of second-rate men—men who always receive it at second-hand. Pedagogues believe in immutable truths and spend their lives trying to determine them and propagate them; the intellectual progress of man consists largely of a concerted effort to block and destroy their enterprise. Nine times out of ten, in the arts as in life, there is actually no truth to be discovered; there is only error to be exposed. In whole departments of human inquiry it seems to me quite unlikely that the truth ever *will* be discovered. Nevertheless, the rubber-stamp thinking of the world always makes the assumption that the exposure of an error is identical with the discovery of the truth—that error and truth are simple opposites. They are nothing of the sort. What the world turns to, when it has been cured of one error, is usually simply another error, and maybe one worse than the first one. This is the whole history of the intellect in brief. The average man of to-day does not believe in precisely the same imbecilities that the Greek of the fourth century before Christ believed in, but the things that he *does* believe in are often quite as idiotic. Perhaps this statement is a bit too sweeping. There is, year by year, a

Footnote on Criticism

gradual accumulation of what may be called, provisionally, truths—there is a slow accretion of ideas that somehow manage to meet all practicable human tests, and so survive. But even so, it is risky to call them absolute truths. All that one may safely say of them is that no one, as yet, has demonstrated that they are errors. Soon or late, if experience teaches us anything, they are likely to succumb too. The profoundest truths of the Middle Ages are now laughed at by schoolboys. The profoundest truths of democracy will be laughed at, a few centuries hence, even by school-teachers.

In the department of esthetics, wherein critics mainly disport themselves, it is almost impossible to think of a so-called truth that shows any sign of being permanently true. The most profound of principles begins to fade and quiver almost as soon as it is stated. But the work of art, as opposed to the theory behind it, has a longer life, particularly if that theory be obscure and questionable, and so cannot be determined accurately. *Hamlet*, the Mona Lisa, *Faust*, *Dixie*, *Parsifal*, *Mother Goose*, *Annabel Lee*, *Huckleberry Finn*—these things, so baffling to pedagogy, so con-

273

tumacious to the categories, so mysterious in purpose and utility—these things live. And why? Because there is in them the flavor of salient, novel and attractive personality, because the quality that shines from them is not that of correct demeanor but that of creative passion, because they pulse and breathe and speak, because they are genuine works of art. So with criticism. Let us forget all the heavy effort to make a science of it; it is a fine art, or nothing. If the critic, retiring to his cell to concoct his treatise upon a book or play or what-not, produces a piece of writing that shows sound structure, and brilliant color, and the flash of new and persuasive ideas, and civilized manners, and the charm of an uncommon personality in free function, then he has given something to the world that is worth having, and sufficiently justified his existence. Is Carlyle's *Frederick* true? Who cares? As well ask if the Parthenon is true, or the C Minor Symphony, or *Wiener Blut*. Let the critic who is an artist leave such necropsies to professors of esthetics, who can no more determine the truth than he can, and will infallibly make it unpleasant and a bore.

Footnote on Criticism

It is, of course, not easy to practice this abstention. Two forces, one within and one without, tend to bring even a Hazlitt or a Huneker under the campus pump. One is the almost universal human susceptibility to messianic delusions—the irresistible tendency of practically every man, once he finds a crowd in front of him, to strut and roll his eyes. The other is the public demand, born of such long familiarity with pedagogical criticism that no other kind is readily conceivable, that the critic teach something as well as say something—in the popular phrase, that he be constructive. Both operate powerfully against his free functioning, and especially the former. He finds it hard to resist the flattery of his customers, however little he may actually esteem it. If he knows anything at all, he knows that his following, like that of every other artist in ideas, is chiefly made up of the congenitally subaltern type of man and woman—natural converts, lodge joiners, me-toos, stragglers after circus parades. It is precious seldom that he ever gets a positive idea out of them; what he usually gets is mere unintelligent ratification. But this troop, despite its obvious failings, corrupts him in various ways. For one thing, it enormously reënforces his belief in his own ideas, and so tends to make him stiff and dogmatic—in brief, precisely everything that he ought not to be. And for another thing, it tends to make him (by a curious contradiction) a bit pliant and politic: he begins to estimate new ideas, not in proportion as they are amusing or beautiful, but in proportion as they are likely to please. So beset, front and rear, he sometimes sinks supinely to the level of a professor, and his subsequent proceedings are interesting no more. The true aim of a critic is certainly not to make converts. He must know that very few of the persons who are susceptible to conversion are worth converting. Their minds are intrinsically flabby and parasitical, and it is certainly not sound sport to agitate minds of that sort. Moreover, the critic must always harbor a grave doubt about most of the ideas that they lap up so greedily—it must occur to him not infrequently, in the silent watches of the night, that much that he writes is sheer buncombe. As I have said, I can't imagine any idea—that is, in the domain of esthetics—that is palpably

Footnote on Criticism

and incontrovertibly sound. All that I am
familiar with, and in particular all that I
announce most vociferously, seem to me to contain a core of quite obvious nonsense. I thus
try to avoid cherishing them too lovingly, and
it always gives me a shiver to see any one else
gobble them at one gulp. Criticism, at bottom,
is indistinguishable from scepticism. Both
launch themselves, the one by esthetic pres-
entations and the other by logical presenta-
tions, at the common human tendency to accept whatever is approved, to take in ideas
ready-made, to be responsive to mere rhetoric
and gesticulation. A critic who believes in
anything absolutely is bound to that something
quite as helplessly as a Christian is bound to
the Freudian garbage in the Book of Revelation. To that extent, at all events, he is
unfree and unintelligent, and hence a bad
critic.

The demand for "constructive" criticism is
based upon the same false assumption that immutable truths exist in the arts, and that the
artist will be improved by being made aware
of them. This notion, whatever the form it
takes, is always absurd—as much so, indeed,

as its brother delusion that the critic, to be
competent, must be a practitioner of the specific art he ventures to deal with, *i.e.*, that a
doctor, to cure a belly-ache, must have a belly-
ache. As practically encountered, it is disin-
genuous as well as absurd, for it comes chiefly
from bad artists who tire of serving as per-
forming monkeys, and crave the greater ease
and safety of sophomores in class. They demand to be taught in order to avoid being
knocked about. In their demand is the theory
that instruction, if they could get it, would
profit them—that they are capable of doing
better work than they do. As a practical matter, I doubt that this is ever true. Bad poets
never actually grow any better; they invariably grow worse and worse. In all history
there has never been, to my knowledge, a single
practitioner of any art who, as a result of
"constructive" criticism, improved his work.
The curse of all the arts, indeed, is the fact
that they are constantly invaded by persons
who are not artists at all—persons whose
yearning to express their ideas and feelings is
unaccompanied by the slightest capacity for
charming expression—in brief, persons with

Footnote on Criticism

absolutely nothing to say. This is particularly true of the art of letters, which interposes very few technical obstacles to the vanity and garrulity of such invaders. Any effort to teach them to write better is an effort wasted, as every editor discovers for himself; they are as incapable of it as they are of jumping over the moon. The only sort of criticism that can deal with them to any profit is the sort that employs them frankly as laboratory animals. It cannot cure them, but it can at least make an amusing and perhaps edifying show of them. It is idle to argue that the good in them is thus destroyed with the bad. The simple answer is that there *is* no good in them. Suppose Poe had wasted his time trying to dredge good work out of Rufus Dawes, author of *Geraldine*. He would have failed miserably —and spoiled a capital essay, still diverting after three-quarters of a century. Suppose Beethoven, dealing with Gottfried Weber, had tried laboriously to make an intelligent music critic of him. How much more apt, useful, and durable the simple note: "Arch-ass! Double-barreled ass!" Here was absolutely sound criticism. Here was a judgment wholly beyond challenge. Moreover, here was a small but perfect work of art.

Upon the low practical value of so-called constructive criticism I can offer testimony out of my own experience. My books are commonly reviewed at great length, and many critics devote themselves to pointing out what they conceive to be my errors, both of fact and of taste. Well, I cannot recall a case in which any suggestion offered by a constructive critic has helped me in the slightest, or even actively interested me. Every such wet-nurse of letters has sought fatuously to make me write in a way differing from that in which the Lord God Almighty, in His infinite wisdom, impels me to write—that is, to make me write stuff which, coming from me, would be as false as an appearance of decency in a Congressman. All the benefits I have ever got from the critics of my work have come from the destructive variety. A hearty slating always does me good, particularly if it be well written. It begins by enlisting my professional respect; it ends by making me examine my ideas coldly in the privacy of my chamber. Not, of course, that I usually revise them, but

Footnote on Criticism

I at least examine them. If I decide to hold fast to them, they are all the dearer to me thereafter, and I expound them with a new passion and plausibility. If, on the contrary, I discern holes in them, I shelve them in a *pianissimo* manner, and set about hatching new ones to take their place. But constructive criticism irritates me. I do not object to being denounced, but I can't abide being school-mastered, especially by men I regard as imbeciles.

I find, as a practicing critic, that very few men who write books are even as tolerant as I am—that most of them, soon or late, show signs of extreme discomfort under criticism, however polite its terms. Perhaps this is why enduring friendships between authors and critics are so rare. All artists, of course, dislike one another more or less, but that dislike seldom rises to implacable enmity, save between opera singer and opera singer, and creative author and critic. Even when the latter two keep up an outward show of good-will, there is always bitter antagonism under the surface. Part of it, I daresay, arises out of the impossible demands of the critic, particularly if he be tinged with the constructive madness.

H. L. Mencken

Having favored an author with his good opinion, he expects the poor fellow to live up to
that good opinion without the slighest compro-
mise or faltering, and this is commonly beyond
human power. He feels that any let-down
compromises *him*—that his hero is stabbing
him in the back, and making him ridiculous—
and this feeling rasps his vanity. The most
bitter of all literary quarrels are those between critics and creative artists, and most
of them arise in just this way. As for the
creative artist, he on his part naturally resents
the critic's air of pedagogical superiority and
he resents it especially when he has an uneasy
feeling that he has fallen short of his best
work, and that the discontent of the critic is
thus justified. Injustice is relatively easy to
bear; what stings is justice. Under it all, of
course, lurks the fact that I began with: the
fact that the critic is himself an artist, and
that his creative impulse, soon or late, is bound
to make him neglect the punctilio. When he
sits down to compose his criticism, his artist
ceases to be a friend, and becomes mere raw
material for his work of art. It is my experience that artists invariably resent this cavalier

Footnote on Criticism

use of them. They are pleased so long as the critic confines himself to the modest business of interpreting them—preferably in terms of their own estimate of themselves—but the moment he proceeds to adorn their theme with variations of his own, the moment he brings new ideas to the enterprise and begins contrasting them with their ideas, that moment they grow restive. It is precisely at this point, of course, that criticism becomes genuine criticism; before that it was mere reviewing. When a critic passes it he loses his friends. By becoming an artist, he becomes the foe of all other artists.

But the transformation, I believe, has good effects upon him: it makes him a better critic. Too much *Gemütlichkeit* is as fatal to criticism as it would be to surgery or politics. When it rages unimpeded it leads inevitably either to a dull professorial sticking on of meaningless labels or to log-rolling, and often it leads to both. One of the most hopeful symptoms of the new *Aufklärung* in the Republic is the revival of acrimony in criticism—the renaissance of the doctrine that esthetic matters are important, and that it is worth the while of

H. L. Mencken

a healthy male to take them seriously, as he
takes business, sport and amour. In the days
when American literature was showing its first
vigorous growth, the native criticism was extraordinarily violent and even vicious; in the
days when American literature swooned upon
the tomb of the Puritan *Kultur* it became
flaccid and childish. The typical critic of the
first era was Poe, as the typical critic of the
second was Howells. Poe carried on his critical jehads with such ferocity that he often
got into law-suits, and sometimes ran no little
risk of having his head cracked. He regarded
literary questions as exigent and momentous.
The lofty aloofness of the don was simply
not in him. When he encountered a book that
seemed to him to be bad, he attacked it almost
as sharply as a Chamber of Commerce would
attack a fanatic preaching free speech, or the
corporation of Trinity Church would attack
Christ. His opponents replied in the same
Berserker manner. Much of Poe's surviving
ill-fame, as a drunkard and dead-beat, is due
to their inordinate denunciations of him.
They were not content to refute him; they constantly tried to dispose of him altogether. The

Footnote on Criticism

very ferocity of that ancient row shows that the native literature, in those days, was in a healthy state. Books of genuine value were produced. Literature always thrives best, in fact, in an atmosphere of hearty strife. Poe, surrounded by admiring professors, never challenged, never aroused to the emotions of revolt, would probably have written poetry indistinguishable from the hollow stuff of, say, Professor George E. Woodberry. It took the persistent (and often grossly unfair and dishonorable) opposition of Griswold *et al*. to stimulate him to his highest endeavors. He needed friends, true enough, but he also needed enemies.

To-day, for the first time in years, there is strife in American criticism, and the Paul Elmer Mores and Hamilton Wright Mabies are no longer able to purr in peace. The instant they fall into stiff professorial attitudes they are challenged, and often with anything but urbanity. The *ex cathedra* manner thus passes out, and free discussion comes in. Heretics lay on boldly, and the professors are forced to make some defense. Often, going further, they attempt counter-attacks. Ears are bitten off. Noses are bloodied. There are wallops both above and below the belt. I am, I need not say, no believer in any magical merit in debate, no matter how free it may be. It certainly does not necessarily establish the truth; both sides, in fact, may be wrong, and they often are. But it at least accomplishes two important effects. On the one hand, it exposes all the cruder fallacies to hostile examination, and so disposes of many of them. And on the other hand, it melodramatizes the business of the critic, and so convinces thousands of bystanders, otherwise quite inert, that criticism is an amusing and instructive art, and that the problems it deals with are important. What men will fight for seems to be worth looking into.

Criticism in the United States [1]

By J. E. SPINGARN

WHEN I wrote the essays which a few years
later were collected in a volume bearing the
subtitle of "Essays on the Unity of Genius
and Taste," the pedants and the professors
were in the ascendant, and it seemed necessary
to emphasize the side of criticism which was
then in danger, the side that is closest to the
art of the creator.   How unimportant it
seemed then to weigh and define all the phases
of a critic's duty, when one of the highest moments of the life of the spirit, the moment of
artistic creation, appeared, at least in America,
to be so completely misunderstood.   But now
the professors have been temporarily routed
by the dilettanti, the amateurs, and the journalists, who treat a work of the imagination

[1] From the article on "Scholarship and Criticism" in
*Civilization in the United States: An Inquiry by Thirty
Americans* (Harcourt, Brace and Company, 1922; preface
dated July 4, 1921), as revised by the author for this
collection. The first section of the article, relating to
scholarship, has been omitted here.

J. E. Spingarn

as if they were describing fireworks or a bull-fight (to use a phrase of Zola's about Gautier); and so it is necessary now to insist on the discipline and illumination of knowledge and thought,—in other words, to write an "Essay on the Divergence of Criticism and Creation."

American criticism, like that of England, but to an even greater extent, suffers from a want of philosophic insight and precision. It has neither inherited nor created a tradition of esthetic thought. Golden utterances there have been aplenty—utterances wise, or acute, or daring enough to confound those who refuse to recognize the American spirit except where they find a faded moralism,—utterances that anticipate the most modern concepts of criticism throughout the world. To this American ancestry of my own thought and that of others I "point with pride." [1] How can we forget Jefferson's literary Declaration of Independence, with its contempt for "the artificial canons of criticism" and its insistence that the only test of literary excellence is whether a work gives pleasure and is "animating, interesting, attaching," even though the idea of

[1] See the Appendix.

pleasure no longer sums up for us the whole spiritual world of art? How can we forget Poe's conception of poetry as "the rhythmical creation of beauty" and of beauty as having "no concern whatever either with Duty or with Truth"; or Emerson's kindred idea that beauty, like truth, is "an ultimate end," and his definition of criticism, with its striking challenge, "Here was a new mind, and it was welcome to a new style"? If we have forgotten them, it is because these utterances have remained more or less isolated, and their implications but half apprehended; they have never been consolidated into a body of thought or imposed themselves as a state of mind on American critics. For virtually all of us every critical problem is a separate problem, a problem in a philosophic vacuum, and so open for discussion to any astute mind with a taste for letters. Realism, classicism, romanticism, imagism, impressionism, expressionism, and other terms or movements as they spring up, seem ultimate realities instead of matters of very subordinate concern to any philosophy of art,—mere practical programmes which bear somewhat the same relation to esthetic truth that the plat-

J. E. Spingarn

form of the Republican Party bears to Aristotle's *Politics* or Marx's *Capital*.

As a result, critics are constantly carrying on a guerilla warfare of their own in favor of some vague literary shibboleth or sociological abstraction, and discovering anew the virtues or vices of individuality, modernity, Puritanism, the romantic spirit or the spirit of the Middle West, the traditions of the pioneer, and so on ad infinitum. This holds true of every school of American criticism, "conservative" or "radical"; for all of them a disconnected body of literary theories takes the place of a real philosophy of art. "Find an idea and then write about it" sums up the average American writer's conception of criticism. There are even those who conceive this scattering of casual thoughts as the sole duty of a critic, on the extraordinary assumption that in this dispersion of thought and power the critic is "expressing himself" as an "artist." Now, while the critic must approach a work of literature without preconceived notion of what that individual work should attempt, he cannot criticize it without some understanding of what all literature attempts. The critic without an esthetic is a mariner without chart, compass, or knowledge of navigation; for the question is not where the ship should go or what cargo it should carry, but whether it is going to arrive at any port at all without sinking.

Criticism is essentially an expression of taste, or that faculty of imaginative sympathy by which the reader or spectator is able to re-live the vision created by the artist. This is the soil without which it cannot flourish; but it attains its end and becomes criticism in the highest sense only when taste is guided by knowledge and rises to the level of thought, for then, and only then, does the critic give us something that the artist as artist cannot give. Of these three elements, implicit in all real criticism, the professors have made light of taste, and have made thought itself subservient to knowledge, while the dilettanti have considered it possible to dispense with both knowledge and thought. But even dilettante criticism is preferable to the dogmatic and intellectualist criticism of the professors, on the same grounds that Sainte-Beuve is superior to Brunetière, or Hazlitt to Francis Jeffrey; for the dilettante at least meets the mind of the artist on the plane of imagination and taste, while the intellectualist or moralist is precluded by his temperament and his theories from ever understanding the primal thrill and purpose of the creative act.

Back of any philosophy of art there must be a philosophy of life, and all esthetic formulæ seem empty unless there is richness of content behind them. The critic, like the poet or the philosopher, has the whole world to range in, and the farther he ranges in it, the better his work will be. Yet this does not mean that criticism, in so far as it remains criticism of the arts of expression, should focus its attention on morals, history, life, instead of on the forms into which the artist transforms them. Art has something else to give us; and to seek moral or economic theories in it is to seek moral or economic theories, but not art. Indeed, the United States is the only civilized country where morals are still in controversy so far as creative literature is concerned; France, Germany, and Italy liberated themselves from this faded obsession long ago; even in England critics of authority hesitate to judge a work of art by moral standards. Yet this is precisely what divides the two chief schools of American criticism, the moralists and the anti-moralists, though even among the latter masquerade some whose only quarrel with the moralists is the nature of the moral standards employed.

The seeds of a more fruitful tradition had been planted in our earlier criticism, as we have seen. But if we disregard the influence of the "new psychology" and of a half-baked "literary anthropology," which has not yet taken definite form, the main forces that have influenced the present clashes in the American attitude toward literature seem to be three. There is first of all the conception of literature as a moral influence, a conception which goes back to the Græco-Roman rhetoricians and moralists, and after pervading English thought from Sidney to Johnson, finds its last stronghold to-day among the American descendants of the Puritans. There is, secondly, the Shavian conception of literature as the most effective instrument for the conversion of the world to a new *Weltanschauung*, to be judged by the novelty and freshness of its ideas, a

J. E. Spingarn

conception particularly attractive to the school of young reformers, radicals, and intellectuals whose interest in the creative imagination is secondary, and whose training in esthetic thought has been negligible; this is merely an obverse of the Puritan moralism, and is tainted by the same fundamental misconception of the meaning of the creative imagination. And there is finally the conception of literature as an external thing, a complex of rhythms, charm, technical skill, beauty without inner content, or mere theatrical effectiveness, which goes back through the English 'nineties to the French 'seventies, when the idea of the spiritual autonomy of art,—that "beauty is its own excuse for being,"—was distorted into the merely mechanical theory of "art for art's sake"; the French have a special talent for narrowing esthetic truths into hard-and-fast formulæ, devoid of their original nucleus of philosophic reality, but all the more effective on this account for universal conquest as practical programmes.

All three of these conceptions have their element of truth, but all three are inadequate and incomplete. Pity the poor esthete for whom art, in any of its single outer manifestations, is the whole life of the spirit; pity the poor moralist for whom the life of the spirit in one of its highest moments is cribbed and confined by a narrow theory of the meaning of life. It may be difficult to tell which of them misses the most; yet who can doubt that when we meet them in practical life the error of the moralist seems the nobler of the two? And how could it be otherwise?—for it is precisely in the life of action that we seek for the guiding star of moral values, which the esthete attempts to evade in assuming that the ideal freedom of the artist as an artist is one with the practical duty of the artist as a man. But in the ideal world of art moralism must always find itself homeless and dispossessed. The very nature of poetry must forever be a bitter challenge to those who have only this narrow single standard; and there is no other way out except that of Plato, who because of the "immorality" of poetry banishes all poets forever from the ideal Republic. Of all the moralistic critics, Plato is the only one who is thoroughly consistent.

The apparent paradox which none of these

J. E. Spingarn

critics face is that the *Weltanschauung* of the creative artist, his moral convictions, his views on intellectual, economic, and other subjects, furnish the content of his work and are at the same time the chief obstacles to his artistic achievement. Out of morals or philosophy he has to make, not morals or philosophy, but poetry; for morals and philosophy are only a part, and a small part, of the whole reality which his imagination has to encompass. The man who is overwhelmed with moral theories and convictions would naturally find it easiest to become a moralist, and moralists are prosaic, not poetic. A man who has strong economic convictions would find it easiest to become an economist or economic reformer, and economics too is the prose of life, not the poetry. A man with a strong philosophic bias would find it easiest to become a pure thinker, and the poet's visionary world topples when laid open to the cold scrutiny of logic. A poet is a human being, and therefore likely to have convictions, prejudices, preconceptions, like other men; but the deeper his interest in them is, the easier it is for him to become a moralist, economist, philosopher, or what not, and the harder for him to transcend them and to become a poet.

But if the genius of the poet (and by poet I mean any writer of imaginative literature) is strong enough, it will transcend them, pass over them by the power of the imagination, which leaves them behind without knowing it. It has been well said that morals are one reality, a poem is another reality, and the illusion consists in thinking them one and the same. The poet's conscience as a man may be satisfied by the illusion, but woe to him if it is not an illusion, for that is what we tell him when we say, "He is a moralist, not a poet." Such a man has merely expressed his moral convictions, instead of *leaping over and beyond them* into that world of the imagination where moral ideas must be interpreted from the standpoint of poetry, or the artistic needs of the characters portrayed, and not by the logical or reality value of morals. When it is said that beauty, like truth, is "an ultimate end," with its implication that in seeking the essential secret of art we must look elsewhere than in its truth or its morals, the utilitarian no less than the narrow moralist assumes that we are giving advice to the dilettante trifler in verse (who

J. E. Spingarn

is not an artist at all) instead of attempting
to define the essential secret of the art of
Æschylus and Dante, Shakespeare and Goethe,
Milton and Racine, and all their high com-
peers, classic and romantic, in the ancient and
modern world. But how can we solve that
secret if we see no difference whatever between
their art and the thought of a Plato or Spinoza,
the moral illumination of an Emerson or
Franklin, or the noble exaltation of the Gettys-
burg Address? The critic who has missed that
difference has missed everything. By ignoring
one of the vital elements necessary to form a
synthesis, he has even missed the power of
understanding their essential unity in the life
of the spirit.

That is what we mean when we say that this
"leaping over" is the test of all art, that it is
inherent in the very nature of the creative
imagination. It explains a myriad problems.
It explains, for example, how Milton the
moralist started out to make Satan a demon
and how Milton the poet ended by making
him a hero; and from this hymning of the devil
we learn how our moralistic critics cannot even
understand a Puritan poet. From another

angle, it explains the blindness of the American critic who recently objected to the "loose thinking" of Carl Sandburg's poem, *Smoke and Steel*, in which steel is conceived as made of "smoke and blood," and who propounded this question to the Walrus and the Carpenter: "How can smoke, the lighter refuse of steel, be one of its constituents, and how can the smoke which drifts away from the chimney and the blood which flows in the steelmaker's veins be correlates in their relation to steel?"

Where shall we match this precious gem? Over two centuries ago, Othello's cry after the death of Desdemona,

> "O heavy hour,
> Methinks it should now be a huge eclipse
> Of sun and moon!"

provoked another intellectualist critic to inquire whether "the sun and moon can both together be so hugely eclipsed in any one heavy hour whatsoever"; but Rymer has been called "the worst critic that ever lived" for applying tests like these to the poetry of Shakespeare. Over a century ago a certain Abbé Morellet,

J. E. Spingarn

unmoved by the music of Chateaubriand's description of the moon,—

"She pours forth in the woods this great secret of melancholy which she loves to recount to the old oaks and the ancient shores of the sea,"—

asked his readers: "How can the melancholy of night be called a secret; and if the moon recounts it, how is it still a secret; and how does she manage to recount it to the old oaks and the ancient shores of the sea rather than to the deep valleys, the mountains, and the rivers?" And so when Macbeth, stung by his agony into immortal eloquence,—"to-morrow and to-morrow and to-morrow,"—finds time but a petty pace that has lighted fools the way to dusty death, and life itself nothing but a tale

"Told by an idiot, full of sound and fury, Signifying nothing,"

can we not imagine some of our own professors, for whom Art is but a pretty page serving King Virtue and Queen Truth, crying out in disdain: "And it is this passage, gentlemen, in which a false and immoral conception of

300

life is expounded, that some of the so-called
esthetic critics consider the high-water mark
of poetry"? Or if we cannot imagine it, it
is only because the passage is not by a modern
poet without the prestige of Shakespeare's
fame.

These are simply exaggerations of the inevitable consequence of subjecting the world
of the imagination to the moods and tests of
actual life. "Sense, sense, nothing but sense!"
cried a great Austrian poet, "as if poetry in
contrast with prose were not always a kind of
divine nonsense. Every poetic image bears
within itself its own certain demonstration that
logic is not the arbitress of art." And Alfieri
spoke for every poet in the world when he said
of himself, "Reasoning and judging are for
me only pure and generous forms of feeling."
The trained economist, philosopher, or moralist, examining the ideas of a poet, is always
likely to say: "These are not clearly thought
out or logical ideas; they are just a poet's
fancy or inspiration"; and the sneer of the
expert may be the final praise of the poet. To
give us a vision of reality, and not reality,
imagination rather than thought or morals,

J. E. Spingarn

is the eternal mission of the artist. To forego that vision is to miss one of the highest moments of the life of the spirit. No other experience can serve as a substitute; no life that has not known it can regard itself as completely fulfilled.

These are some of the elementary reasons why those who demand of the poet a definite code of morals or manners, the ready-made standards of any society, however great, that is bounded by space or time—"American ideals," or "Puritanism," or on the other side, "radical ideas"—seem to me to show their incompetence as critics. Life, teeming life, with all its ardors and agonies, is the only limit within which the poet's vision can be cabined and confined; and all we ask of him is that he create a new life in which the imagination can breathe and move as naturally as our practical selves can live in the world of reality. How can we expect illumination from those who share the "typical American business man's" inherent inability to live in the world of fantasy which the poets have created, without the business man's ability to face the external facts of life and mold them to his will?

Criticism in the United States

These men are schoolmasters, pedants, moralists, policemen, but neither critics nor true lovers of the spiritual food that art provides. To the creative writers of America I should give a wholly different message from theirs. I should say to them: "Express what is in you, all that serene or turbulent vision of multitudinous life which is yours by right of imagination, trusting in your own power to achieve discipline and mastery, and leave the discussion of 'American ideals' to statesmen, historians, and philosophers, with the certainty that if you truly express the vision that is in you, the statesmen, historians, and philosophers of the future will point to your work as a fine expression of the 'American ideals' you have helped to create. Do not wait for the flux of time to create a society that you can copy, but create your own society; and if you are a great writer it will be a Great Society, which the world will never cease to live in and to love. For you America must always be not old but new, something unrealized, something to be created and to be given as an incredible gift to a hundred million men. Courage is the birthright of the poet as much as of the soldier or statesman; and courage in trusting your imagination is to you the very breath of life. But mastery of the imagination, and not mere submission to it, must be your goal; for how can the true artist express himself in terms of slavery rather than power? By giving what is best in him to his art, the American artist serves America best."

A profound inner reform is needed in order that the critics of America may prepare themselves adequately to interpret this new literature, to separate the chaff from the wheat, and in so doing to purify and ennoble the taste and enlarge the imaginative sympathies of a whole people.

The first need of American criticism to-day is education in esthetic thinking. It needs above all the cleansing and stimulating power of an intellectual bath. Only the drenching discipline that comes from mastery of the problems of esthetic thought can train us for the duty of interpreting the American literature of the future. The anarchy of impressionism is a natural reaction against the mechanical theories and jejune text-books of the professors, but it is a temporary haven and not a home. The haphazard empiricism of English criticism and the faded moralism of some of our own will serve us no more. We must desert these muddy waters, and seek purer and deeper streams. For the conception of the critic as megaphone or phonograph we must substitute the conception of the critic as esthetic thinker. In a country where philosophers urge men to cease thinking, it may be the task of the critic to revivify and reorganize thought.

The second need of American criticism can be summed up in the word scholarship—that discipline of knowledge which will give us at one and the same time a wider international outlook and a deeper national insight. One will spring from the other, for the timid Colonial spirit finds no place in the heart of the citizen of the world; and respect for native talent, born of a surer knowledge, will prevent us alike from overrating its merits and from holding it too cheap. For the lifeless pedantry of the professors, who think that tradition actually lives in monuments, heirlooms, dead ancestors, and printed books, we must substitute the illumination of a humane scholarship,

which realizes that learning is but a quest for
the larger self and that tradition is a state of
the soul. Half-knowledge is either too timid
or too cocksure; and only out of the spiritual
discipline that is born of intellectual travail
and adventure can come a true independence
of judgment and taste.

For taste is after all both the point of departure and the goal; and the third and greatest need of American criticism is a deeper sensibility, a more complete submission to the
imaginative will of the artist, before attempting to rise above it into the realm of judgment.
The critic is not a man seated on a block of
ice watching a bright fire, or how could he
realize the full force of its warmth and power?
If there is anything that American life can be
said to give least of all, it is training in taste.
There is a deadness of artistic feeling, which
is sometimes replaced or disguised by a fervor
of sociological obsession, but this is no substitute for the faculty of imaginative sympathy
which is at the heart of all criticism. By taste,
I mean, of course, not the "good taste" of the
dilettante or the amateur collector, or taste in
its eighteenth-century sense, but that creative

moment of the life of the spirit which the artist and the enjoyer of art share alike. For this the ardor of the reformer, the insight of the historian, even the moral passion of the saint is no substitute; for taste, or esthetic enjoyment, is the only gateway to the critic's judgment, and over it is a flaming signpost, "Critic, abandon all hope when this gate is shut."

This is your task, critics of America—to see that Plato's dream of banishing poets from the ideal Republic does not come true. It is your chief duty, against moralist and hedonist and utilitarian alike, to justify the ways of beauty to Americans. In a land where virtuous platitudes have so often been mistaken for poetry, it is your task to explain the real meaning of the esthetic moment for the higher lives of men. But no one knows better than I that you cannot rest satisfied even with this. For the modern critic has learnt to distinguish clearly between art, philosophy, history, religion, morals, not for the purpose of denying but of establishing their essential unity in the life of the spirit. Those who deny this unity and those who would substitute for it a mud-

dle-headed if well-meaning confusion are alike
the Enemy. Though you reject the criticism
in which beauty is forever measured and tested
by the moralist's rigid rules and justified by
virtues that are not her own, still less can you
be satisfied with the criticism in which "ideas"
are struck out in random and irresponsible
flashes like sparks from the anvil of a gnome.
You cannot be satisfied with anything but
truth—that whole truth which is life—even
in the service of beauty.

Ku Klux Kriticism [1]

By ERNEST BOYD

LITERARY criticism in this country has, at least, the charm of consistent irrelevancy. With English criticism it shares, of course, the fundamental irrelevancy of the moral, as opposed to the esthetic standard, and is only happy when confronted with literature that is both morally and esthetically good. In the absence of the latter quality the Anglo-Saxon critic, with rare exceptions, is consoled by the former, but in the absence of the former he is so incensed that one naturally draws the inference that the apparent appreciation of the beautiful, of the esthetically perfect, is really conditioned by an appeal to the "moral sense." Benedetto Croce has lived in vain, so far as these worthy arbiters are concerned, as his most prominent American champion recently discovered when

[1] Originally published in *The Nation* (New York), June 20, 1923, and revised by the author for this collection.

Ernest Boyd

he had to remind an eminent professor that it was not the immoral and Mediterranean Croce, but the blond and Nordic Emerson who declared that "beauty is its own excuse for being."

By way of counteracting this school of criticism America has gradually evolved an opposition partly founded upon the equally irrelevant doctrine that whatever is radical is good. The term "radical" is accepted in the widest and most abusive sense employed by the stupidest conservatives, and may include defiance of the Seventh Commandment and the Eighteenth Amendment, a belief in the Declaration of Independence and the Single Tax, the nationalization of industry and One Big Union. In consequence of this curious readiness to make their own whatever bogies haunt the dreams of their sleepiest adversaries, the left wing extends an affecting tolerance to all literature, however execrable in style and construction, which seems to challenge the existing order. The story of an adultery is admirable, provided it be self-conscious and sordid. If an author has sound views concerning the League of Nations and the release of polit-

Ku Klux Kriticism

ical prisoners his work is assured of an enthusiastic reception at the hands of critics who would scorn the same naïvetés and crude workmanship in a Harold Bell Wright.

Thus the two schools of opinion into which American criticism falls are moved primarily by considerations that are irrelevant to the understanding and appreciation of art. Conservatives of the caliber of George Saintsbury and Anatole France are as rare amongst American critics as are radicals like Georg Brandes. Between the two extremes are a few isolated figures whose influence is as nothing beside that of another and peculiarly indigenous type of criticism which has never quite decided to which school it belongs. These are those influential journalists who write of books with the enthusiasm of auctioneers and speak of them with the tongues of traveling salesmen. They would probably—and certainly rightly —describe themselves as "regular fellows," and they make their standards accordingly. When not preoccupied with the more substantial delights of baseball and poker they emerge to pronounce their emphatic conviction that whatever volume they have last read "sure is

311

Ernest Boyd

some book." These obiter dicta make countless thousands rejoice, and publishers mourn whose wares do not happen to have received this invaluable advertisement. Praise and blame are showered upon the just and the unjust alike, without regard for the possible ethical or esthetic merits or demerits of the works in question. The only author who is certain never to benefit by this apparent impartiality is the author of genuine original talent who has no friends at court. These critics, while emancipated to some degree from the irrelevant considerations that hamper their conservative and radical colleagues, are innocent of critical background and utterly without a sense of values other than news values.

In the circumstances it is not surprising that, while a national literature of considerable interest and vitality is growing up in America, American criticism is proving inadequate to the tasks that concern it. In the arts, as in the life of America itself, the same process of growth and evolution is going on, and it is producing results which are curiously parallel. The Ku Klux Klan has its counterpart in Ku Klux Kriticism. It is not the least of the

Ku Klux Kriticism

charms of the American scene that ideas once current in influential circles are immediately reflected in mob action. The hooded hooligans who lynch and flog to the greater glory of their Nordic and Protestant God are merely the large scale product of doctrines more discreetly evolved by their betters—dolichocephalic democracy. In all its manifestations the Ku Klux spirit derives its impulse from the resentment provoked by the obvious fact that America is not an Anglo-Saxon country, that numerous infiltrations of race and culture are gradually creating for this country a national identity which is not that of the Colonists, whose names are so often taken in vain. The situation is aggravated by the persistent emergence in every field of American life of these sinister "aliens" who have completely forgotten—if they ever knew it—the tradition which relegated them to subordinate occupations. The new national literature, in particular, would shrink to its old provincial status with remarkable rapidity if the literary lynching bees could only eliminate those names which have not the familiar Anglo-Saxon ring, or do not stand for those ideas which one unconscious

313

Ernest Boyd

humorist has designated "the genius of America."

Hence the rise of Ku Klux Kriticism, which
would see to it that American literature be
Nordic, Protestant, and blond. One does not
expect an intelligible or reasoned confession
of faith from the exponents of this democratic
method of grappling with national problems;
theirs is not to reason why but to do . . . and
make the other fellow die. The Ku Kluxers
of criticism are, in this respect, true to type,
for the most part. They content themselves
with a general denial of the right of any person
whose name seems "foreign" to speak on behalf of America. One of their number, however, has undertaken a more or less coherent
exposition of the ideas and ideals that animate
the Klan in its literary operations. In his volume, *On Contemporary Literature*, Professor
Stuart Sherman arrives at the crescendo of
his appreciation of Mark Twain in a phrase
which is at once an illuminating irrelevancy
and a declaration of the Ku Klux faith: in
impassioned italics he exclaims that Mark
Twain *"was an American."* Then, feeling,
perhaps, that this admirable virtue hardly

Ku Klux Kriticism

seems adequate as a summary of the qualities which entitle Mark Twain to his position in American literature, Professor Sherman continues: "To the foreign critic this ultimate tribute may seem perplexingly cheap and anticlimactic. That is, of course, due to the mistaken notion that we number some fivescore millions of Americans. As a matter of fact, we number our Americans on our ten fingers; the rest of us are merely citizens of the United States. Any one who will take the trouble to be born may become a citizen. To become an American requires other talents."

This metaphysical and ingenuous distinction between "Americans" and "citizens of the United States" is an attempt to rationalize the position of the Ku Klux Klan. Its fundamental assumption is that America is not a nation in the process of evolution, drawing its life from the various races that are helping to build it up, but an Anglo-Saxon colony unfortunately afflicted by the influx of aliens. In "Americans" the same critic carries his theory a step further by explicitly recognizing the heterogeneous character of the American people and as explicitly rejecting these, to him, exotic elements in its composition. "This latest generation of Americans," he writes, "so vulgar and selfish and good-humored and sensual and impudent, shows little trace of the once dominant Puritan stock and nothing of the Puritan temper. It is curiously and richly composed of the children of parents who dedicated themselves to accumulation and, toiling inarticulately in shop and field, in forest and mine, never fully mastered the English definite article or the personal pronoun. It is composed of children whose parents or grandparents brought their copper kettles from Russia, tilled the soil of Hungary, taught the Mosaic law in Poland, cut Irish turf, ground optical glass in Germany, dispensed Bavarian beer, or fished for mackerel around the Skagerrack." No exception need be taken to this more or less accurate illustration of the development of America. What is interesting is the typical Ku Klux revolt against the implications and consequences of this development.

The professors of blond Nordic literature hold this new generation responsible for all the ills which, in their opinion, infest the republic of letters. The writers who disturb their aca-

demic calm bear names suggestive of those
lesser breeds whose parental history Professor
Sherman has outlined. The critics who champion this new literature are similarly tainted,
and its public is exclusively composed of the
newly emancipated children of once humble
slaves. Of the critics we are told that "however it may be connected with the house of
Jesse," it is not a group "which should be expected to hear any profound murmurings of
ancestral voices or to experience any mysterious inflowing of national experience in medi-
tating on the names of Mark Twain, Whitman,
Thoreau, Lincoln, Emerson, Franklin and
Bradford." As for the readers whose tastes
are guided by these critics, they revel in "the
English paradoxers and mountebanks, the
Scandinavian misanthropes, the German ego-
maniacs, and, above all, in the later Russian
novelists, crazy with war, taxes, hunger, anarchy, vodka and German philosophy." Here
is heard the raucous note of the Know Nothing movement, the instinctive revolt of the
mandarin against "foreign devils," with, of
course, the inevitable echo of belated English
controversies concerning Ibsen and Strindberg

Ernest Boyd

and Nietzsche. Be Anglo-Saxon or be forever silent is the exhortation of the critical
Ku Klux to the false prophets of Americanism, whose heresy it is that in this great welter
of races and creeds and cultures the "ancestral voices" of only one group should not be
heard.

The alternative to what has been facetiously
named "the Loyal Independent Order of
United Hiberno-German-Anti-English Americans" is a mysterious something described as
"essential Americanism," which automatically
excludes whole races and traditions which are
becoming, in an essentially American manner,
an integral part of America. Emerson, it
seems, was wrong when he uttered his immoral
dictum concerning Beauty, for, in spite of "ancestral voices," Professor Sherman did not recognize its Anglo-Saxon authenticity. In place
of what appeared to be a characteristically perverse sentiment, inspired by vodka or German
egomania in those who are undermining the
Puritan stamina of America, he substituted the
statement that "beauty has a heart full of
service." Thence it followed that art in America must serve the community; it must justify

318

its existence to the philistines who argue that business is the proper study of man. The dominant characteristic of the American genius is "an incomparably profound moral idealism." Incomparably profound moral idealism, by definition, however, is the privilege of only a fraction of the peoples who constitute the American nation, and it is this fraction which is alone entitled to be heard.

There is something refreshingly naïve in this appeal to the artist on behalf of the community when from that community is excluded many of its inseparable elements. What if these dangerous tribes, with their background of Russian copper kettles, Irish turf and Bavarian beer, regard this new literature in which they collabôrate as readers and writers as the true expression of the American genius of which they are a part? It is not the artist who is responsible to the community, but rather the community which must give the artist the material of which his dreams are made. This America is a much more complicated and less homogeneous entity than is dreamt of in the philosophy of the Ku Klux and its literary counterpart. It might be more profitable to

Ernest Boyd

ascertain to what degree that "vulgar and selfish and good-humored and sensual and impudent" new generation is expressed by the artists and critics whom it supports than to attempt to rehabilitate the Puritan, as Professor Sherman does, by proving him to have been what he was not, to an age that is entirely uninterested in such speculations. It may well be that precisely between this new literature and this new generation there exists that relation based upon mutual interpretation and comprehension which is the only possible relation between the artist and the community.

Appendix

*Passages Illustrating the Growth of an American
Tradition of Criticism* [1]

"I have always very much despised the artificial
canons of criticism. When I have read a work in
prose or poetry, or seen a painting, a statue, etc., I
have only asked myself whether it gives me pleasure,
whether it is animating, interesting, attaching. If it
is, it is good for these reasons."—THOMAS JEFFERSON
(letter to William Wirt, November 12, 1816.)

"When I told Alcott that I would not criticize his
compositions; that it would be as absurd to require
them to conform to my way of writing and aiming,
as it would be to reject Wordsworth because he was
wholly unlike Campbell; that here was a new mind,
and it was welcome to a new style; he replied, well
pleased, 'That is criticism.'"—EMERSON (*Journals*,
1838).

"Beauty is its own excuse for being."—EMERSON.

"This element [Beauty] I call an ultimate end.
No reason can be asked or given why the soul seeks
beauty. Beauty, in its largest and profoundest sense,

[1] See page 288.

321

Appendix

is one expression for the universe. . . . Like Truth, it is an ultimate aim of the human being."—EMERSON.

"There is then creative reading as well as creative writing. . . . Why should we write dramas, and epics, and sonnets, and novels in two volumes? Why not write as variously as we dress and think?"—EMERSON.

"The only proper method of testing the merits of a poem is by measuring its capabilities of exciting the Poetic Sentiments in others."—POE (1836).

"I would define, in brief, the Poetry of words as the Rhythmical Creation of Beauty. Its sole arbiter is Taste. With the Intellect or with the Conscience, it has only collateral relations. Unless incidentally, it has no concern whatever either with Duty or with Truth."—POE.

"A heresy which, in the brief period it has already endured, may be said to have accomplished more in the corruption of our Poetical Literature than all its other enemies combined. I allude to the heresy of The Didactic. It has been assumed that the ultimate object of all Poetry is Truth. Every poem, it is said, should inculcate a moral, and by this moral is the poetical merit of the work to be adjudged. . . . But the simple fact is that would we but permit ourselves to look into our own souls, we should immediately there discover that under the sun there neither exists nor can exist any work more thoroughly dignified,

Appendix

more supremely noble than this very poem, this poem
per se, this poem which is a poem and nothing more,
this poem written solely for the poem's sake."—Poe.

"To the reviewer [his] duty is the plainest,—the
duty not even of appreciation, or of censure, or of
silence, at his own will, but at the sway of those sentiments and of those opinions which are derived from
the author himself, through the medium of his written
and published words. True criticism is the reflection
of the thing criticized upon the spirit of the critic.
. . . In fact, to appreciate thoroughly the work of
what we call genius is to possess all the genius by
which the work was produced."—Poe.

"Excellence may be considered an axiom, or a prop-
osition which becomes self-evident just in proportion
to the clearness or precision with which it is put. If
it fairly exists, in this sense, it requires no further
elucidation. To point out too particularly the beauties of a work is to admit tacitly that these beauties
are not wholly admirable. Regarding, then, excellence as that which is capable of self-manifestation,
it but remains for the critic to show when, where, and
how it fails in becoming manifest."—Poe.

"The Boston critics, who have a notion that poets
are porpoises (for they are always talking about their
running in 'schools') cannot make up their minds as
to what particular school he must belong."—Poe.

"Following the highest authority, we would wish,
in a word, to limit literary criticism to comment upon

Appendix

Art. A book is written—and it is only *as the book* that we subject it to review. With the opinions of the work, considered otherwise than in their relation to the work itself, the critic has really nothing to do. It is his part simply to decide upon *the mode* in which these opinions are brought to bear. Criticism is thus no 'test of opinion.' For this test, the work, divested of its pretensions as an *art-product*, is turned over for discussion . . . if a history, to the historian, if a metaphysical treatise, to the moralist."—Poe (1842).

"There is no just and serene criticism as yet. Our taste is too delicate and particular. It says nay to the poet's work, but never says yea to his hope."—Thoreau.

"Who that has heard a strain of music feared then lest he should speak extravagantly any more forever?"—Thoreau.

"They [the highest type of critics] enter into the nature of another being and judge his work by its own law. But having done so, having ascertained his design and the degree of his success in fulfilling it, they do also know how to put that aim in its place and how to estimate its relations. . . . Finally the critic is worthy to judge."—Margaret Fuller (*Papers on Literature and Art*, 1846).

"What suits Great Britain . . . does not suit a mixed race, continually enriched with new blood from other stocks the most unlike that of our first descent,

Appendix

with ample field and verge enough to range in and leave every impulse free, and abundant opportunity to develop a genius, wide and full as our rivers, luxuriant and impassioned as our vast prairies, rooted in strength as the rocks on which the Puritan fathers landed. . . . That day will not rise till the fusion of races among us is more complete."—Margaret Fuller (essay on American Literature, 1846).

"Lowell [as a writer of verse] is absolutely wanting in the true spirit and tone of poesy. His interest in the moral questions of the day has supplied the want of vitality in himself. . . . To those who cannot understand the voice of Nature or Poetry, unless it speak in apothegms, and tag each story with a moral, I have nothing to say."—Margaret Fuller (1846).

"The top of the hill he will ne'er come nigh reaching
    Till he learns the distinction 'twixt singing and
        preaching."
                                    James Russell Lowell
                            (criticism of his own poetry, 1848).

"What difference would it make in our judgment of Hamlet or Othello if a manuscript of Shakespeare's memoirs should turn up, and we should find out that he had been a pitiful fellow? None in the world; for he is not a professed moralist, and his life does not give the warrant to his words. . . . This is precisely the difference between what appeals to our esthetic or to our moral sense, between what is judged of by our taste or by our conscience."—James Russell Lowell.

Appendix

"Art, in itself considered, is neither moral nor immoral. It belongs to an entirely separate class of things."—JAMES C. MOFFAT (*Introduction to the Study of Æsthetics*, 1856).

"Allons! from all formulas!
From your formulas, O bat-eyed and materialistic priests!

.   .   .   .   .

Brain of the New World! what a task is thine!
To formulate the Modern.—Out of the peerless grandeur of the modern,
Out of Thyself—comprising Science—to recast Poems, Churches, Art,
(Recast—maybe discard them, end them—Maybe their work is done—who knows?)
By vision, hand, conception, on the background of the mighty past, the dead,
To limn, with absolute faith, the mighty living present."

—WALT WHITMAN.

"These two processes [reasoning and judgment] have no power over Beauty; and if falsely applied to this idea, they immediately destroy it in its own peculiar nature, and confound it with some ideas of which they can take cognizance, as utility and fitness. . . . The faculty, the mental power which arrives at this attribute [Beauty] is an internal intuition."—JOHN BASCOM (*Æsthetics*, 1862).

"Oh, rest assured that there are no stereotyped forms of poetry. It is a vital power and may assume any guise and take any shape."—HENRY TIMROD (1863).

Appendix

"That pallid and emasculate scholarship of which New England has furnished too many examples."—FRANCIS PARKMAN.

"We do not condemn a creative work when it departs from some rule or precedent, but when it violates its own principle, when it is not consistent with itself, when it hath not eyes to see, or ears to hear, or hands to reach what lies within its own sphere."—JOHN BURROUGHS.

"It [morality] is in reality simply a part of the essential richness of inspiration—it has nothing to do with the artistic process and it has everything to do with the artistic effect. . . . Be the morality false or true, the writer's deference to it greets us as a kind of essential perfume."—HENRY JAMES (1884).

"What is the meaning of your morality and your conscious moral purpose? Will you not define your terms and explain how (a novel being a picture) a picture can be either moral or immoral? You wish to paint a moral picture or carve a moral statue: will you not tell us how you would set about it? We are discussing the Art of Fiction; questions of art are questions (in the widest sense) of execution; questions of morality are quite another affair; and will you not let us see how it is that you find it so easy to mix them up? . . . The essence of moral energy is to survey the whole field. . . . No good novel will ever proceed from a superficial mind; that seems to me an axiom which, for the artist in fiction, will cover all needful moral ground."—HENRY JAMES (1888).

Appendix

"The only obligation to which in advance we may hold a novel . . . is that it be interesting. . . . The ways in which it is at liberty to accomplish this result . . . are as various as the temperament of man. . . . A novel is in its broadest sense a personal, a direct impression of life: that, to begin with, constitutes its value, which is greater or less according to the intensity of the impression. But there will be no intensity at all, and therefore no value, unless there is freedom to feel and say. The tracing of a line to be followed, of a tone to be taken, of a form to be filled out, is a limitation of that freedom and a suppression of the very thing that we are most curious about."—HENRY JAMES (1888).

"For myself I live, live intensely and am fed by life, and my value, whatever it be, is in my own kind of expression of that."—HENRY JAMES (1915).

"If I were authorized to address any word directly to our novelists, I should say: Do not trouble yourself about standards or ideals, but try to be faithful and natural. . . ."—WILLIAM DEAN HOWELLS.

"I do not like to have you say that the supreme art in literature made you set art forever below humanity. The antithesis is not correct. There is no common measure. Is not Art, properly understood, the expression of humanity? What you mean by it here, I presume, is the technical method which it is the aim of so-called artists to acquire, the 'art' to which men devote themselves at the cost it may be of their humanity; but not the art of the great artists

Appendix

through whom Nature has uttered the voice of the world."—CHARLES ELIOT NORTON (letter to W. D. Howells).

"Nothing seemed more certain than that the American people were not artistic, that they had as a people little instinct of beauty; but their intelligence in its higher as in its lower forms was both quick and refined."—HENRY ADAMS (*History of the United States during the Second Administration of James Madison*, 1890).

"In no other critic will esthetic perceptions and moral convictions be found presented with less real confusion of esthetic and moral ideals."—FERRIS GREENSLET (*James Russell Lowell*, 1905).

"What profit was it, you asked, to take an author whose writing is filled with the subtlest appreciation of the world's beauty, and stretch him on the rack of a harsh ethical theory? Pater was a lover and confessor of strange souls; should not, then, a true critic come to him in the same receptive mood? Well, I dare say you were right."—PAUL ELMER MORE (*The Drift of Romanticism*, 1913, prefatory letter to Frank Jewett Mather, Jr.).

"Personally I don't care a rap whether we call the Flight of a Tartar Tribe, or certain passages in the Confessions of an Opium Eater, prose or vers libres. I enjoy Wordsworth's sonnets and I enjoy Shakespeare's sonnets; and I don't care in the least if some one proves to me that Shakespeare did not write sonnets but something else."—THEODORE ROOSEVELT.

Appendix

"The naughty boy theory and practice of criticism, with its doling out of bad marks."—JAMES HUNEKER.

"Poe is just as American as Mark Twain; Lanier is just as American as Whittier. Professor Van Dyke says that Poe was a maker of 'decidedly un-American cameos,' but I do not understand what that means." —JOHN MACY (*The Spirit of American Literature*, 1913).

"Art, true Art, is the desire of man to express himself, to record the reactions of his personality to the world he lives in."—AMY LOWELL.

"I can only repeat that art is not a branch of pedagogy."—JAMES BRANCH CABELL.

THE END